DISCOVER YOUR PASSION FOR TEENS

A 30-Day Course That Will Change Your Life!

GAIL A. CASSIDY

BALBOA.PRESS

A DIVISION OF HAY HOUSE

Balboa Press books may be ordered through booksellers or by contacting:

Balboa Press
A Division of Hay House
1663 Liberty Drive
Bloomington, IN 47403
www.balboapress.com
1 (877) 407-4847

Because of the dynamic nature of the Internet, any web addresses or links contained in this book may have changed since publication and may no longer be valid. The views expressed in this work are solely those of the author and do not necessarily reflect the views of the publisher, and the publisher hereby disclaims any responsibility for them.

The author of this book does not dispense medical advice or prescribe the use of any technique as a form of treatment for physical, emotional, or medical problems without the advice of a physician, either directly or indirectly. The intent of the author is only to offer information of a general nature to help you in your quest for emotional and spiritual well-being. In the event you use any of the information in this book for yourself, which is your constitutional right, the author and the publisher assume no responsibility for your actions.

Any people depicted in stock imagery provided by Getty Images are models, and such images are being used for illustrative purposes only.
Certain stock imagery © Getty Images.

ISBN: 978-1-9822-4834-5 (sc)
ISBN: 978-1-9822-4835-2 (e)

Library of Congress Control Number: 2020909913

Print information available on the last page.

Balboa Press rev. date: 06/12/2020

DEDICATION

To my family—You are the best!!
To my husband, Tom, thanks for allowing me to follow my passion.

ABOUT THE AUTHOR

Gail Cassidy, author and educator, has developed programs for high school students, educators, IBM, The American Red Cross, an international training corporation, school administrators in Lithuania and others.

Her current concentration is on encouraging leaders to incorporate training, which provides validation, direction, and communication skills for teens and young adults in order to reduce dropout rates, violence, and bullying, while increasing the maximization of each participant's potential. Kindness does count.

Gail A. Cassidy

CONTENTS

SECTION 6 - HELPFUL RESOURCES, SUCCESS TEAMS, COACHING

SECTION 7 - JOB SEARCH PREPARATION INTERVIEWING

SECTION 8 - SIX STEPS TO SUCCESS

SECTION ONE

INTRODUCTION

INTRODUCTION FOR TEACHERS AND STUDENTS

The Laws of Human Nature were addressed in the first of the three recommended courses to increase every student's self-esteem. That course is the Speaking Skills for Teens course, the second part of what is needed for high school students is direction. This course is an 8-week elective, preferably for juniors. Each student is special, and this course zeros in on what makes each one special and how that knowledge can help them plan their futures.

Computerized aptitude tests are frequently used to determine careers in which students may be successful. *Discover Your Passion for Teens* takes a different approach. On a computerized test, a student must choose one answer, e.g. your favorite color. If their favorite color isn't listed, the test is skewed, albeit ever so slightly.

With the exercises in *Discover Your Passion,* students are asked questions they can discuss with their peers, and there are never any wrong answers. These sessions are opportunities for insightful thinking for each student taking this elective.

Wouldn't it be nice if everyone could do what they wanted to do every day and still earn money? How great would it be to feel excited when you awaken every morning? Wouldn't everyone like to feel that what they do makes a difference in the world?

All of this is possible once a person knows what his or her passion is and knows how to put that passion to work. Master motivator and author, Barbara Sher, says it best in the title of her book, *I Would Do What I Love If Only I Knew What It Was.*

By the last session of this elective, students will know not only what their passion is but also have ideas about how to earn money pursuing that passion whether it is full-time or as an income-producing hobby.

Obviously, no two people are alike. Everyone has unique talents, knowledge, skills, and abilities. Finding which skill, which bit of knowledge, or which talent a person most enjoys using will lead to discovering their passion.

Wayne Dyer says, "There is no scarcity of opportunity to make a living at what you love; there's only a scarcity of resolve to make it happen. Even Oprah says, "Your job is to discover what your true calling is." Therein lies your happiness.

Discover Your Passion for Teens was written to help students discover their passion and earn money doing what they love. The four major objectives of this program are

1. to help them clarify their passion or path,
2. to prepare them for a job search or help some of the students to find their business,

3. to familiarize them with marketing basics, and
4. to help them learn how to make their dreams come true. Students can progress at their own rate or work in small groups.

Some sessions will take longer than others. Students will enjoy this journey, whether they are headed to college or to a vocational school to master a skill or to go out and find a job.

The program is designed to allow each participant to recognize what is special about themselves and to find a direction in life. The information students glean from their responses are important pieces necessary to complete their jigsaw passion puzzle. Fit them all together and they will have their passion.

THE IMPORTANCE OF HAVING A PURPOSE

Victor Frankl in his book, *Man's Search for Meaning,* describes his horror-filled days as a prisoner in a Nazi prison camp. He said he made an interesting observation about those people who survived the terror and hardships of their ordeals.

He stated, in effect, that those who had a purpose in life survived; those who did not see any hope or believe they a purpose, died, even if physiologically equal. That is a significant observation.

Similarly, Wayne Dyer in *Real Magic* recalls the words of the prison inmate, "Nothing is more likely to help a person overcome or endure troubles than the consciousness of having a task in life."

Altering his words a bit by using the word *passion* in place of *task,* would read *"Nothing is more likely to help a person overcome or endure troubles than the consciousness of having a passion in life."* That is what teachers want students to uncover as they progress through this course.

The #1 deadly fear of many people is having lived a meaningless life. My husband started his own business many years ago, because, as he said, he didn't want to wake up on his deathbed and say to himself, "I should have given it a shot."

"The only courage you ever need is the courage to live your heart's desire." -Oprah

Now is the time!!! This course is the way!!!

In her e-zine, Barbara Sher, author of *Wishcraft,* wrote **"You're all obligated to do what you love because that's where your gifts lie and those gifts belong to all of us."**

Implicit in that statement are **three premises:**

1. everyone is here for a purpose, and
2. everyone is here to help others, and

3. gravitating toward pleasure, e.g., doing what you love, is not only okay, it is mandatory if you want to help others and if you are seeking the wonderful illusives called happiness, satisfaction, and serenity.

"The time to be happy is now; the place to be happy is here, and the way to be happy is by helping others." - Charles Englehardt. That says it all.

Now that the students are in high school, the time has come for them to discover how to use their gifts to make the world a better place. By doing so, they will not only enrich their lives but also the lives of others. This is an opportunity to make the world a better place.

In each of these three course books, students will find the baker's dozen of essential human nature laws. Teachers cannot just tell others to show respect to get respect, be non-judgmental, etc. **They need a way for kids to experience these laws and hopefully adopt them.**

These three separate courses—*Speaking for Teens, Kids Mentoring Kids,* and *Discover Your Passion for Teens*—"show" rather than "tell" the laws of human nature with the intent of having them "buy in."

This one course, ***Discover Your Passion for Teens,*** is the opportunity for teens to study themselves without judgment and make decisions based on what they experience in the course.

The importance of belief! Napoleon Hill wrote in his book *Think and Grow Rich*: "What the mind can see **and** believe, it can achieve."

The concept is still the same; it's still true -- if a student's mind can think up or conceive of an idea and believe in it, he can achieve it.

If you believe you can do something, what's stopping you? What have you gotten to believe that acts as an obstacle to your success? Do you believe you can't "get" math, you can't make friends, you aren't bright, you can't sing, you are clumsy, etc." Some may be true, and that's fine. The point is, if you believe it, you act accordingly.

A person might **want** to be a singer, but if they can't carry a tune, they're not going to believe they can be a singer. Maybe they're horrible in math. If so, they're probably not going to WANT to be a scientist or an engineer, but they may be great in something else.

"If your mind can conceive and believe in doing something, you can achieve it. If you believe you can, what's stopping you? What have you gotten to believe that acts as an obstacle to your success?"

A favorite saying is from Henry Ford, the founder of Ford motors and the first assembly line for the manufacture of cars. He said, "If you think you can or you think you can't, you're right." **"If you think you can or if you think you can't, you're right."**

"Belief applies not only to human beings, but also to the animal kingdom, even insects.

EXAMPLE # 1: If you catch flees and put them in a jar, they will jump up and hit their heads, jump up and hit their heads on the lid until finally they believe they can't get out. So, they sit on the bottom of the jar.

You can take the lid off of the jar, you can move the jar around, upside down, and the flees will not jump again. Why? Because they believe they can't get out. The point is: the flea comes to believe he cannot escape, even when the route to escape is clear; therefore, in his head, he cannot escape. That's how strong belief is.

EXAMPLE #2: Now, from a much larger point of view is that of an elephant. You may see a baby elephant tied with a thin chain that goes around his leg and is attached to a stake in the ground. The elephant gets bigger and bigger and bigger, and finally there is this huge pachyderm who is tied to a stake in the ground with a little, thin chain. Obviously, he could just move it, pull his foot up, take it away; but he doesn't because—he believes he can't. He won't do what he can't believe he can do. This is the power of belief.

Like the elephants, many of us, especially kids, go through life hanging onto a belief that we cannot do something, simply because we failed at it once before.

EXAMPLE #3: Another example is Dr. Herbert Benson, a researcher from Harvard University. He was involved with a meditation movement way back when transcendental meditation first became popular. Benson spent his career studying, among other things, meditation and the mind. He traveled to Tibet and observed how the mind can be trained as evidenced by the spiritual men and the monks could sit on a mountain top dressed in only a loincloth covered with a sheet and have the snow melt that fell onto the sheet.

From years of intense prayer and solitude, these monks were mentally capable of raising their body temperatures.

In some tribes, Dr. Benson found that the shaman or the medicine man could point to somebody after a trial and say, "Go home and die," and the person went home and died because he believed so strongly in the shaman—again, the power of belief!

If you think you can or you think you can't, you're right.

Frequently, kids believe they're incapable in some manner, who believe they're not accepted, who believe the teachers are being unfair to them. Some of their beliefs might be true, but they must be listened to and encouraged."

The point is our beliefs determine our success or lack of success in life. Kids need to know they are worthwhile, that they have something to offer the world. Everybody does, but sometimes talent is just not utilized because a person doesn't believe in the existence of that talent.

Our beliefs guide us as it does our students.

ANOTHER EXAMPLE OF BELIEFS: Sometimes beliefs have a tremendous effect on a person of any age. For two summers the author had taught school administrators in Lithuania. This country had been under Russian rule for 50 years and had been subjected to considerable destruction, including their educational system. An American organization, A.P.P.L.E. (American Professional Partnership for Lithuanian Education) was founded and worked with teachers for 25 years before disbanding. American instructors worked with school teachers and administrators to teach them the latest ways that Americans do things in order to try to help them get their education system up to par.

The teachers had some beliefs that are different than what Americans were used to.

In the classrooms, there was no air-conditioning. On one hot day, I (author) opened a window and opened the door to get a cross breeze. Immediately, one of the ladies immediately got up and closed the window or closed the door. I then reopened the window and reopened the door, and they would say with fear in their voices, "No, no, you can't do that because if you sit in a draft, you'll get a cold and possibly die."

They believed what they said! They believed if they sat in a draft, they would die. I could not deny their wishes.

When I first got married, my mother-in-law was horrified that I washed my hair at night and went to bed. She believed I would die. I would get a cold and die. She believed that.

What beliefs do you, the reader, have about yourself, about your background? Are they positive or negative?

I always thought I couldn't go to college because "a nice Irish girl didn't run away from home" and "You're too big for your britches." That's what my father told me, but I believed I could go to college and pay for it myself, and I did.

What about your abilities? Do you believe you're good in math? Do you believe you're good in English? Do you believe you're good in science? Do you believe you're good in physical education? Can you sing? Can you dance? What are your beliefs about yourself physically, mentally, spiritually? Those beliefs determine how you do in life.

The simple, although not always easy, answer is: all you have to do is change those negative beliefs or have somebody point out to you what your strengths are. It's amazing when somebody hits the nail right on the head. You know it; they know it.

Every person has strengths and weaknesses. In this course, Discover Your Passion, there are exercises that enable each student to find theirs; and, along the way, may find their life's work. Keep in mind, there are no wrong answers!

Every person has strengths and weaknesses. In this course, *Discover Your Passion for Teens,* there are exercises that enable each student to find theirs; and, along the way, may find their life's work. Keep in mind, there are no wrong answers!

Gail A. Cassidy

SESSION ONE

(For Teachers and Students)

Do you wish you that when you graduate that could do what you wanted to do every day and still earn money? For me, my passion was teaching and still is. Would you like to feel excited when you awaken every morning? Would you like to feel that what you do makes a difference in the world?

All of this is possible once you know what your passion is and know how to put that passion to work. Master motivator and author, Barbara Sher, says it best in the title of her book, *I Would Do What I Love If Only I Knew What It Was.* By Session 30, you will have a good idea what your passion is but also how to earn money pursuing that passion.

No two people are alike. Everyone has unique talents, knowledge, skills, and abilities. Finding which skill, which bit of knowledge, or which talent you most enjoy using will lead you to your passion. Wayne Dyer says, "There is no scarcity of opportunity to make a living at what you love; there's only a scarcity of resolve to make it happen. As mentioned previously, even Oprah says, "Your job is to discover what your true calling is." Therein lies your happiness.

Welcome to *Discover Your Passion for Teens*, a thirty-session course to help teens discover their passion and in the future earn money doing what they love.

The four major objectives of this program are (1) to help teens clarify their passion, (2) to prepare them for a job search or help them find their future business, 3) to familiarize teens with marketing basics, and 4) to help them learn how to make their dreams come true.

Please have your students progress at their own rate. The major lesson divisions are according to the information regarding the topic. Some sessions will take longer than others. Take your time and enjoy the journey.

Progress at your own rate. There are 30 sessions. Obviously, some sessions will take longer to complete than others. The beginning lessons consist primarily of background information to help them in their search for their passion. Students may want to keep their answers together in a notebook in order to make their analysis easier at the end.

The information students glean from their responses will be important pieces necessary to complete their jigsaw passion puzzle. Fit them all together and they will have their passion.

(In order to simplify reading, the author has chosen to switch between the use of male and female pronouns rather than constantly writing him/her and will frequently use "you" in place of "teens" or "students".)

Section Three consists of invaluable Internal and External Tools for Success. These tools can be used for far more than the information in this book. They can be applied to any problem-solving or decision-making situation in life.

Section Four covers the selection of a potential Profit Center.

Section Five details General Marketing recommendations.

Section Six outlines Helpful Resources and a primer on Human Relation skills.

Section Seven contains Job Search Preparation and a brief primer on Interviewing Skills.

Section Eight addresses the Six Steps to Success, the Pathway to Your Dreams.

Enjoy the program. You and your students are studying the best, most interesting subject possible--yourself!

BACKGROUND: How the Course Came About

Is That All There Is?

The quest for my passion began in 1986 when I was working in a wonderful, well known, worldwide, non-profit agency. Every day I dealt with disasters, fires, floods, AIDS, homeless people, abused children, and other very depressing segments of life.

I found that I could not divorce myself from my work. I hurt with every client I served. I took their problems and negative feelings home with me. It did not take long before I knew I had to get away from this barrage of calamities and disasters happening in other people's lives. That's when I started reading every book I could find on finding my purpose in life.

By the way, my successor handles these same challenges wonderfully. I could not. This job, to her, is her passion. She can turn off the job at 5:00 and go home to her family.

During my tenure at this agency, singer Peggy Lee's haunting refrain rang in my head, "Is that all there is? Is that all there is? Is that all there is, my friend?" I first heard this song when I was in my 20's; then it was nothing more than a popular song I sang along with.

Those single years were fun-filled, career-driven, opportunity-laden times crammed with working and dating and finally marrying "Mr. Right." There was neither time nor inclination to wonder if I were making a difference in the world or even if I were on the right path.

I hummed along to the lilting tune in my 30's, the years that saw me tending babies, decorating a new home, cooking, cleaning, raising children, and making ends meet. I was too busy and too tired to do anything but live in the present, where I heard the constant refrains: "She hit me!" "Don't touch!"

"Sit down." "No!" "Yes." "I'll count to three." "Please - stop - screaming!" These were my daily tunes. Hugs and kisses were my rewards, and life was exactly as it should have been.

It was not until my 40's that the implication of that refrain struck me. "Is that all there is?" This is it? My two challenging and rewarding careers in my 20's were great. Delightful part time jobs as I raised my children were fun. My kids and husband were my existence in my 30's and 40's.

The children grew up and are now wonderful adults, and my husband has become more and more immersed in his own activities. Now what? Is this it? "Is that all there is?"

During my early 40's, a friend and I attended the funeral of an elderly gentleman who had lived an incredibly successful life. He had numerous inventions and patents to his credit. He had initiated a philanthropic organization, and he had left a large, wealthy, caring family. Indeed, to our minds, he had truly left his footprints in the sands of time. The eulogies for him were magnificent--effusive in their praise of his life--and up-lifting.

On the way out of the church, my friend, who is one of the sweetest, most caring ladies I have ever known and who is also a fantastic cook, said in a depressed voice, "What have I done in life? My tombstone will read, 'Here lies Marge. She made a great meatloaf.'" I chuckled. She didn't.

For me, this was the turning point, the event that triggered my intense search to find my passion.

For some reason, her comment stayed in my mind, and the more I thought about it, the more I realized that Marge, indeed, has make a difference on this planet, doing what she does best. She is the one who has taken care of people who were in need. It was she who made people feel special on their birthdays and holidays through her kindness and her cooking. What she considered mundane, her friends recognized as truly special

The point, however, **is** that while others may think what you do is special, you have to also; otherwise, you will never feel as if you are living the life you should be living. **You have to feel that your life has been fulfilled in some way.** And you can, if you believe you have fulfilled your passion. First, however, you have to discover it.

You, too, may have been told "You are such a great <u>(fill in the blank)</u>, but that does nothing for you. For example, my daughter is very talented artistically, and I have frequently asked her why she doesn't do more with her talent. Recently she replied, "I really don't enjoy drawing or painting." So even if you have a talent, you may not enjoy utilizing what seems obvious to those close to you. Others cannot determine your passion; only you can.

You have to focus on what will fulfill you. **Your goal is to find a life's work that inspires passion and earns you money.** One that sustains energy. One that seduces you. One that won't leave you alone. One which you think about wherever you are, whatever you are doing.

In Stephen Pollan's book, *Second Acts,* he writes, "When you keep your dreams locked away in inner darkness, they begin to wear away at your soul. But, by exposing those repressed dreams to the light and pursuing them, you lift your soul to unimaginable heights. Simply by raising the curtain on your Second Act, giving yourself the possibility of a new life, you'll experience more joy and contentment than you can imagine. A Second Act doesn't just change the specific aspect of your life that you're reinventing; it invigorates your entire life."

When you discover your life's work, you will realize that you already have the gift to make it happen.

You won't passionately desire to be an opera singer if you can't carry a tune. Life is not that unfair. Nature is not capricious.

Life has endowed us with the ability, even if unknown to us at the present moment, to fulfill the mission for which we were put on this earth.

In *O Magazine* Oprah said, "It's an irrefutable law of the universe: You always get exactly what you intend--and my intention was to be seen by others as the dependable one, even if that came as a high expense to me personally."

In the same article she wrote, "A business student of mine once challenged me on this concept. 'I'm passionate about cooking,' she explained, 'but my parents have spent nearly $100,000 on my education. For me to now announce that I want to cook....How can I change my mind?'

"I said, 'Is $100,000 worth a life not fulfilled? How much of your life will you have to consume before you can please *you*?'"

Before you get too excited, I do have a RECOMMENDATION: If you are working right now, don't quit your job, and certainly don't quit school!! I quit my full time job after I formally studied to be a coach, after I knew that I wanted to write, teach, and coach people about maximizing their potential, and after I had sufficient funds to get by for at least six months.

If you follow the schedule and the directions in this manual, you should not only have a good idea of what your passion is, but also know how you can begin working on it and also making money at it.

My second recommendation is to listen to your heart, not to the advice of others. I promise you that if you make a choice that doesn't please your folks, your friends, your aunt, or anyone else, the world will not fall apart--the people who truly love you want you to love yourself and love what you do every day. And as you become more clear about who you really are, you'll be better able to decide what is best for you and, therefore, best for everyone who cares for you.

"Every day passion speaks to us through our feelings. That's why, when you allow yourself to become anesthetized by what others think, you literally block yourself from living the life you were called to live." -Oprah.

As Kahlil Gibran said many years ago, "If you cannot work with love, but only with distaste, it is better that you should leave your work and sit at the gate of the temple and take alms of those who work with joy." His statement may be taking discovering your passion too far, but it is an interesting thought.

Specifically, what you can expect at the end of the course are the following four things:

(1) Statement of Passion
(2) Future choice of a college major or employment Idea
(3) Plan
(4) Implementation Process

They are the primary purposes of this course: for students to find fulfillment in their lives and be able to be financially solvent.

Gail A. Cassidy

ASSIGNMENT: Complete the following four Inventory Questions.

INVENTORY QUESTION #1:

1. **What do you like to hear said about you?**

Think of the compliments you have received in your lifetime. Which ones were most meaningful to you?

Do you like to hear that you are bright, innovative, independent, strong, funny, reliable, honest, good looking, prosperous, caring, loving, kind, etc.?

Suppose you are being introduced at a meeting 20 years from now. How would you like to be introduced? Write out your future introduction.

INVENTORY QUESTION #2

What childhood memory and/or achievement gives you the greatest pleasure to recall?

Did you ever receive a special prize--sports award, dancing award, perfect attendance award . . .? Did you ever have your name in the paper or receive a special letter from someone?

It may help to find your favorite childhood memory first. In your mind, review each grade since kindergarten. Think of the teacher, the lessons you took, the people you played with as a child, the sports you played. Then think about what you are most proud of insofar as recognition of an achievement is concerned.

Write as many memories and achievements as you can recall. Use a separate page, if necessary. It may help you to think of time periods in your life:

- ages 1-5

- 6-10

- 11-15

- 16-20

- 21-30

- 31-40

- 41-50

- 51-90

(If older, continue to complete Column 2)

What special memories jump out for each of these periods? Write as many as you can think of.

INVENTORY QUESTION #3

Look at the memories and achievements you have listed for each age group and zero in on WHY the memory is memorable. Is it because you used a special skill or talent or that you received recognition/ validation or did it just made you feel special?

What is so special about each memory and achievement?

Did you become aware of some aspect of yourself that you were unaware of, e.g., a capability or talent or skill? Did you like to build things, take things apart, draw, sing, dance, make up stories, cook……….

List what you learned about each memory/recognition:

-
-
-
-
-
-
-

SESSION TWO

SELF-ASSESSMENT (know where you are now)

Before you begin any major undertaking, you first want to make sure you have a need to do what you intend to do. Your responses on the following assessment will help clarify for you why you are taking this program.

If you answer "YES" to at least 10 of the following questions, then this course is for you!

- Would you like to be drawn into, energized, and fulfilled by your future career?
- Would you like to awaken each workday morning excited about the day?
- Would you like to live the adage, "Do what you love and you will never have to work another day in your life?
- Would you want to do every day what you love doing in your spare time?
- Do you agree with Wayne Dyer's statement, "What you believe enables you to bring that belief into your life and see it?"
- Do you believe in Marsha Sinetar's book title that says, *Do What You Love, the Money Will Follow?*
- Do you believe in Buddha's primary recommendation for achieving enlightenment which is "discovering your right livelihood?"
- Do you believe in and value your intuition?
- Do you believe that your self-esteem increases drastically when you have found your right niche, recognized it, and acted on it?
- Did you know that the number one deadly fear, according to the authors of *Repacking Your Bags*, is having lived a meaningless life?
- Do you subscribe to the wisdom in Englehardt's quote, "The time to be happy is now; the place to be happy is here; the way to be happy is by helping others?"
- Do you believe a life's work inspires passion?
- Do you believe that when you discover your life's work you will realize you already have the gift to make it happen?
- Do you believe in the value of relaxation and visualization?
- Would you like to learn more about yourself?
- Are you interested in analyzing your experiences, talents, knowledge, and skills?
- Would you like to know what your purpose in life is?

How did you do? Write your number of "yes's" here _____.

You can look back at this number this time next year and see if you have reason to change it.

If you have a part-time job right now, evaluate your current job satisfaction.

Does your job allow you to do the following:

- fulfill your goals and objectives?
- have a sense of being appreciated for what you do?
- work on the tasks you most enjoy and/or are most proficient at?
- maintain your personal and professional values and beliefs?

If you answered "No" to any of the above, you would want to make changes either within the context of your job or outside the context of our job. First jobs are usually not greatly satisfying. You probably have it in order to earn some extra money, and that's it!

If you were working full-time, your first step would be to talk to the person for whom you work. Is it possible to work together on goals and objectives? Statistically, less than 50% of workers know the expectations of their bosses. This may be a time to attempt to remedy the situation and, at the same time, incorporate the tasks you most enjoy doing or at which you are most proficient. Again, these ideas may not be applicable to you at this time.

Lack of appreciation or violation of your personal and professional values is a major red flag--time to go! But first, let's take a look at what "passion" is, why this course is invaluable for you, the importance of having a purpose, and the benefits of this particular program.

SESSION THREE

WHAT IS A *PASSION*?

Passion is a realization of yourself. It is who you are. It is what brings you joy. It is your purpose in life.

Your passion could be loving to make money; it could be helping the homeless or inventing a new product. It could be anything you love doing, anything that gives you tremendous satisfaction. And, ironically, your passion in practice has a favorable impact on others.

You don't have to save the world; you don't have to take any unusual courses; you just have to be as you are and do what comes naturally. If you want to be a doctor or nurse or accountant, etc., courses, training, studying would be necessary to do what you most want to do. Finding your passion and fulfilling it makes the learning pleasurable.

Your passion could be performing a certain task or doing something in a certain way. For example, my husband has his own small, one-man business which allows him to go into the office when he wants to, work out when he wants to, be home when he wants to, attend the kids' sporting activities, and basically control his own hours--to him, that is paramount. He works the hours he wants to work-- night, weekends, days--and that is freedom; that is what he most desires. His passion is not related to the products he sells. His passion is utilizing his natural humor and personality to brighten the lives of his customers, and all while earning money and having the freedom to work the hours he desires to work. Making people feel good is something he does easily and naturally.

A passion could result from many things:

- **Possessing a talent**--artist, singer, dancer, writer.
- **A circumstance**, such as losing a children to a drunken driver, that led to the formation of MADD, Mother's Against Drunken Driving; suffering from a medical disease that led to Michael J. Fox's devotion to finding a cure for Parkinson's Disease; experiencing a disabling spinal cord problem led to Christopher Reeve's dedication to stem cell research when he was alive.
- **A desire**--a fascination with how something works or how something is done.
- **A need**--to help others, to nurture, to make a difference.
- **A recognition** of the values most important to you.
- **An accidental incident** to which you are exposed, witnessing poverty situations in the world or land-mine use or abuse of children or the elderly, or unfairness or lack of equality. The list of possibilities is endless.

AND a passion is not cast in concrete. What you are passionate about today may change as the circumstances in your life change. You are not born with a stamp on your forehead that reads "doctor,"

Remember, discovering your passion means discovering what you love to do and can do with tremendous happiness and satisfaction. Your passion at age 15 may have been to perform as a gymnast; at age 40, it may be coaching gymnasts or broadcasting the events or writing about them--same passion--different delivery systems or methods of being involved.

Answer these two questions in order to have a baseline from which to start:

1. **Why are you seeking your passion? (List every reason you can think of.)**

2. **What would it mean to you if you knew your passion? E.g., how would your life be different than it is now?**

In an article from John Agno's newsletter, Coach2Coach, Agno writes about Po Bronson's book. *What is Your Life Work or LifeSignature?* He writes:

> "Remember, as a young child, when you believed that you could change the world? Where are those dreams and aspirations of youth? You may feel you are now ready for a life makeover but are not sure what the changes should be. But you know you want more than what is.

> **"Personal and business success starts with answering the question: "What should I do with my life?"**

Po Bronson, who also wrote *What Should I Do With My Life?* (Random House), tells us that some people keep from finding themselves because they feel guilty for simply taking this question seriously. Many people feel guilty for obsessing about what kind of work they should do. It feels self-indulgent. Yet, people succeed by unleashing a productive, creative and focused energy that flows from the inside-out to work at things they love doing.

> "We live in an economy where we don't have to tolerate jobs we hate. For the most part, we get to choose. But that choice isn't about a job search so much as an identify quest. So, don't be cursed because of your tremendous ability and infinite choice of jobs. Decide what you can devote your life to and then live your dream.

> **"There are too many smart, educated, talented people operating at a slow speed in jobs they are just tolerating.**

> "They have put their dream in a lock box so they could go out and make a ton of money to support the big house, the fancy car, the summer/winter place, the private schools, etc. The unfortunate outcome of following this path is that they become

emotionally invested in that world--and don't really want to ditch it by opening up the lock box and letting their dream surface.

"The shortest route to living the good life involves building the confidence that you can live happily within your means. Sure, it's scary to imagine living on less. But embracing your dream is surprisingly liberating. Instilled with a sense of purpose, your spending habits naturally reorganize because you discover that you need less.

"Sooner or later, we all yearn to break out of our secure harbors.

"The heart moves beyond the familiar and convenient into more adventurous realms of possibility. If we don't break out, our future will always remain in the hands of someone else...not as something we claim fully as our own. Living our life with a deeper understanding that draws us to realize our ideals, walk our talk, and act in accord with what we know to be true is to live your dream.

"Leaders move people by articulating a dream they hold that elicits optimism, compassion or a sense of connection--aspirations that point toward a hopeful future. Resonance flows from a leader who expresses feelings with conviction because those emotions are clearly authentic, rooted in deeply held values."

THREE QUESTIONS:

1. **To what extent do you relate to this article?**
2. **From reading this article, what has "hit" you or resonated with you?**
3. **What can you put to use immediately? Write it down here so you don't lose it.**

WHY THIS COURSE IS INVALUABLE TO YOU

After childhood and required education is completed, people frequently develop an "itch," a yen, to find their purpose or niche in the world, a desire to make a difference. This commonly-held feeling is reflected in our world today where people have moved beyond the necessities of survival, safety, and self-esteem. With those needs having been met, people want/need to move to the next level of life. You now have the opportunity to do now what others do later in life.

Those who are struggling to survive are not going to be interested in this program. They are interested in putting a meal on the table and a roof over their heads. They are motivated by survival and safety. That is their passion. Once those necessities are fulfilled, they, too, will want to move to the next level.

Many of you are ready to take the first step, the step to self-fulfillment or *self-actualization*, as Maslow would say.

On **Maslow's Hierarchy of Human Needs,** you are probably at the #4 or #5 position. If that is where you are, then you won't be satisfied until you have found your own special niche in the world, which, by the way, does not mean there is only one niche for you.

1. **Physiological/Survival**
2. **Safety**
3. **Belongingness/Social**
4. **Esteem/Ego Status**
5. **Self-Actualization**

The #1 deadly fear of many people is having lived a meaningless life. Again, my husband started his own business because he didn't want to wake up on his deathbed and say to himself, "I should have given it a shot."

Even when people are about to retire, it is never to late to find their passion NOW! In fact, it's even more fun in retirement, where life's challenges are different, where retirees have more freedom to do as they please. If you are in high school, now is the perfect time to start this incredible journey.

Jot down brief answers to the following three questions:

• **At this point, what do you believe your purpose is?**

• **How do you know?**

• **How does your passion differ from what you're doing now?**

THE BENEFITS OF TAKING THIS PROGRAM

Do you believe in the statement "Do what you love and never have to work another day in your life."

Think about it. Delve into what you already do in your spare time. *(I used to develop programs in areas I was interested in but at which I was not proficient, for example, children's activities, children's parties, hypnosis, DYP, weight loss. Then one day it hit me--I've always developed programs--back to my first teaching days, then IBM, Dale Carnegie, then Red Cross, and now).*

What greater gift can there be than having a good time doing what you love every day!

Discovering your passion and then doing it will bring you more satisfaction and happiness than all of the money and power in the world.

• *A friend of mine was very successful in the computer cable field, felt he was getting no satisfaction, so he sold his company and is devoting himself to his passion--golf--more specifically, golf etiquette. He wrote a booklet on the subject and is selling it to golf courses along the East Coast of the U.S.*

People need to know they are making a difference. Feeling as if you are being taken for granted or feeling as if what you do doesn't count results in a lack of desire to work to your maximum.

Have you experienced these feelings?

Finding and working your passion can eliminate negativity. Read what the experts have to say.

- Wayne Dyer, in *Believing It Is Seeing It* explains that what you believe enables you to bring that belief into your life and see it. This is why it is so important to discover your passion and believe you can follow that passion.
- Marsha Sinetar wrote a book called *Do What You Love, The Money Will Follow.* That title says it all.
- Edward James Almos, the actor, as a commencement speaker, said, "One more thing before we leave. Please never, ever work for money. Please don't just get a job. A job is something that many of you had in order to earn extra money. A job is something you do for money. But a career is something you do because you're inspired to do it. You want to do it. And you would do it even if you were paid nothing beyond food and the basics. You'd do it because it's your life."
- Life is not a dress rehearsal. We should do what we were meant to do on earth.
- For teachers who tutor on the side, this course will help you help your clients discover their passion and help you find another center of profit.
- In Sarah Breathnach's book, *Simple Abundance*, she says that one of Buddha's primary recommendations for achieving enlightenment is discovering your right livelihood.
- Doing what you love allows you to experience less negative stress, and at the same time experience a different exhilarating type of stress.

OTHER BENEFITS:

- Working your passion will give you a life filled with wonder, excitement, contentment, satisfaction, delight.
- You will experience an increase in self-esteem because you know you are making a difference.
- Singer Naomi Judd said, "I'm a simple, practical person. My theory is, decide where your passions lie, where you can do the most good, then just get involved.
- Denis Waitly in an article, "Chase Your Passion (Not Your Pension)", in *Priorities* magazine said, "By letting money pursue you but never catch you, you'll always be its master. By always doing what you love, loving what you do, delivering more than you promise, you'll always be underpaid--which is how it always should be."
- Essayist Carlyle wrote: "Blessed is he who has found his work; let him ask no other blessedness."

EXAMPLES OF PEOPLE WHO PURSUED THEIR PASSION:

- Jack Lemmon was 9 when he was a last-minute replacement in a play, an event that gave him direction for the rest of his life.
- Bob Scuban was an electrician. He sold his company and took lessons to become a sea captain.
- A lady in one of my classes loved quilting. She also loved researching people's genealogies. She combined the two and started a business where she researches the person's genealogy and then designs a quilt pattern and teaches the person how to do it.
- As I wrote before, my husband loves his business because of the freedom it allows him and the satisfaction he receives from his interactions with his customers. He meets his friends for breakfast at 8:00 every day, works in his office from until noon, then goes to the Y, then lunch, and is back in the office until 5:30. He may also work all evening and weekends, but that is his choice. He has want he wants—income, freedom, and personal satisfaction. He is blessed with a personality and sense of humor that enables him to make people's lives better each day whether through business or pleasure. It is something he does easily and effortlessly, just as your passion is something that comes naturally to you.

Key Point: Doing what you love makes you and the world a better place.

QUESTION: WHAT BENEFITS DO YOU SEE BY DOING WHAT YOU LOVE?

SESSION FOUR

Complete questions 4 – 6.

EXPLANATION: Inventory Question #4 is significant because you are relying on your senses to respond. It could be a *feeling* or a *smell* that you respond to. Your response could be due to colors. Some places *feel* exciting or relaxing or stimulating or comfortable. No logic is necessary here. It is strictly feeling.

On the next page you have columns to choose from. Do you like working indoors, outdoors, or home or a combination of each?

Do you like lots of people around, few people, structured 9 - 5 jobs or unstructured, self-starter positions?

Do you like small towns, city life, rural life?

Think of the places where you enjoy being: airports, malls, hotels, museums, etc. Each has a *feel* for you. Concentrate on each location and see how you react to it. Does it *feel* right?

Engage all of your senses when you think about each location.

I love the *smell* of schools, but I don't like the *feel* of libraries. I like the *sounds* in a mall, but not the *sounds* or *smells* of a museum. I love the *feel* of elegance at a hotel and the *feeling of excitement* at a city hall or courthouse.

Add places that come to mind where you enjoy being. There are no right or wrong answers, only answers that pleasure your senses.

INVENTORY QUESTION #4:

Where do you most enjoy being?

PLACES TO WORK

Where do you love to be?

Put a check next to each location that *feels* right to you Be more specific where possible. Add a location, if it is not here.

WHERE	WHAT	SIZE/POSITION
• Indoors	School/College	Large Small
	Library	
	Hospital	
	Bank	
	Court	
	Office building	
	Museum	
	Hotel	
	Computer technology	
	Factory	
	Airport	
	Studio	
	Restaurant	
	Mall	
	Retail store:	Buyer
	Books	Owner
	Sales	
	Housewares	
	Crafts Shop	
	Hardware	
	Pet store	
• Outdoors	Construction	Other:
	Forester	
	Landscaper	
	Travel guide	
	Garden center	
	Zoo	
	Sports	
	Real Estate	

| • Home | Consulting | Other: |
| | Creative | Caterer |

• Organizational style	Plush	Other:
	Formal	
	Informal	• Location:
	Alone	Small town
	Lots of people	City
	Few people	Rural area
	Unstructured, e.g. sales	Other
	Structured, 9 - 5 in office	

EXPLANATION: INVENTORY QUESTIONS #5 & #6:

Inventory question #5 relates to "Internal Values," the values that steer your actions on a daily basis. These values usually don't change throughout your life, unless you consciously attempt to incorporate them into your life. Internal values are the steering mechanism in your brain.

In Inventory Question #6, External Values are values that frequently do change over the years. As a teenager, *beauty* and *pleasure* may be paramount. As a person matures, *family* may become number one priority. As kids leave the nest, they are not less important, but are not focused on in the same way.

Good health, peace of mind, and *freedom* may work themselves toward the top of your list. If they do, be prepared to accept the responsibility that comes with each. Are you willing to change your eating habits, your exercise habits? Are you willing to consciously work on eliminating stressors in your life in order to possess peace of mind? What price will you pay for more freedom--less money, smaller home, older car . . .?

Choosing the values is the simple part. The challenge comes with recognizing that each choice comes with a price, either in time, energy or money. The prizes however are the gifts of your choices.

Please note that if any of your basic internal values conflict with your job, you will not be happy. If *integrity* is high on your list and you are forced to "cook the books" or do something less than honest, you will be quite unhappy. If you love cheerfulness and the atmosphere is gloomy, you will be miserable. If "family" is most important to you, traveling 300 days a year will be a conflict for you, resulting in unhappiness.

Gail A. Cassidy

INVENTORY QUESTION #5: Circle the internal values you feel are most important to you or those you would like to be a part of you, if they currently are not. Circle as many as you would like.

INTERNAL VALUES

Values That Steer Your Daily Actions
VALUES THAT REMAIN STABLE ALL THROUGH LIFE

Honesty
Courage
Peacefulness
Self-reliance
Discipline
Friendship
Work
Faith
Morality
Ethics
Moderation
Fidelity
Loyalty
Dependability
Respect
Unselfishness
Sensitivity
Kindness
Friendliness
Justice
Mercy
Sincerity
Integrity
Compassion
Fairness
Cheerfulness
Independence
Perseverance
Religion
Spirituality
Responsibility
Reliability

INVENTORY QUESTION #6: Circle your 3 most important external values. There are no incorrect selections.

<u>**EXTERNAL VALUES**</u>

VALUES THAT MAY CHANGE AS YOU PROGRESS IN LIFE (in contrast to internal values such as honesty and integrity, which generally do not change as you progress in life)

<u>**Things Most Important to You Now**</u>

Creativity	Artistic expression
Acceptance	Second home
Admiration	Companionship
Emotional well-being	Family
Education	Being loved
Physically challenging	Recognition
Wisdom	Comfort
Appearance	Fitness
Beauty	Encouragement
Approval	Easy work
Love	Excitement
Friendship	Freedom
Service to others	Prestige
Security	Wealth
Fulfillment	Pleasure
Self actualization	Money (financial security)
Status	Privacy
Power/leadership	Pets
Fun	Interesting work
Pleasant environment	Challenging work
Travel	Work close to home
Material satisfaction	Longevity
Peace of mind	Retirement
Good health	Free time
Fame	Respect from others

SESSION FIVE

Complete the final nine questions:

INVENTORY QUESTION #7:
Analyze your reading preferences and habits:

Books: When you go into a bookstore, which section do you go to first? Look at your home bookshelves. What types of book do you buy?

Magazines: If you were taking a long air flight, what magazines would you bring with you? In those magazines, which articles would you definitely read and which would you skip?

Newspapers: If there were only one section of the paper that you could read, which section would it be--financial, headlines, crossword puzzle, local news, world news?

Other: What other types of reading material do you enjoy?

INVENTORY QUESTION #8 explanation:

The inventory question on the next page is very significant. Think of everything you enjoy doing in your spare time. If you say "watching television," of what significance is that, you may ask? I think of Rosie O'Donnell, who devoted herself to television as a child and, as a result, became so familiar with and knowledgeable about the programs that she made a career out of television.

"Shopping" you say. Did you ever hear of the Professional Secret Shoppers? In Nordstroms Department stores, people are hired to shop for others or at least consult with them on their purchases.

In addition to television and shopping, most people have something they enjoy--traveling, cooking, building birdhouses, painting, organizing. Is your house immaculate? Organizing may be your niche. *Haley's Hints* was written by someone who loved organizing. The book contains over 2,000 of the most extraordinary money- and time-saving uses for ordinary household items. Haley's passion is obviously to make life easier, so he collected his ideas and put them into writing to make life easier for others.

If you had no television and no car (in the shop being repaired, ergo, keeping you from shopping), what would you do in your spare time?

Give this a lot of thought. You may overlook what you do as insignificant. Nothing is insignificant.

INVENTORY QUESTION #8:

What do you most enjoy doing in your spare time?

Think about the hobbies you pursue, the tasks you most enjoy, the places you visit. Do you like to write, read, cook, travel, shop, play sports, be around sports or theater or schools/colleges. If you could anything you wanted in your spare time, what would it be?

Another way to look at this question is to answer "What is **FUN** for me? For example, when my son was young, he delivered newspapers early in the morning in order to earn enough money to buy models—cars, planes, etc,—which he enjoyed putting together. He and his friend built a go-cart using an old lawn mower engine and odd and end materials to assemble the cart. He could figure out how to put anything together—that was fun for him. His major in college: engineering.

INVENTORY QUESTION #9: What do you do easily, naturally?

What comes easy to you? Do you make friends easily? Is speaking in front of a class easy for you? Can you whistle, sing, dance, draw, write? Can you entertain your friends with ease? Can you pick out the right colors, fabrics, and accessories? Think of everything you can that is not difficult for you to do and that you enjoy doing.

This is a difficult question because frequently people do things so easily they assume everyone can do the same. For example, my daughter is a very talented artist, yet she would not list that as something special because it comes naturally to her. That is why it is good to ask people who know you well what they think you do easily and naturally.

INVENTORY QUESTION #10:

The next Inventory Question is more of a process of elimination. Cross out those things you do not like to do. That automatically narrows your career or niche choices.

Add whatever skill comes to mind, if it is not listed. You may find a pattern develop here when you study those things you crossed out. For example, anything to do with math or finance I would cross out. That automatically eliminates numerous careers for me.

A pattern may also develop that leans towards helping others or organizing or leading or solving or doing physical vs. mental things. See what patterns develop for you.

INVENTORY QUESTION #10: Which skills do you most enjoy using?

SAMPLE SKILLS
(Circle those skills that most interest you.)

Achieving goals	Engineering	Measuring	Repairing
Administrating	Entertaining	Mechanical	Researching &
Advertising	Evaluating	Mediating	Representing
Agriculture	Experimenting	Monitoring	Science
Analyzing	Financial	Motivating	Selling
Artistic	Fund raising	Naturalist	Simplifying
Banking	Grants writing	Negotiating	Social Service
Cleaning	Graphic arts	Numerical	Solving Problems
Clerical	Growing things	Nurturing	Supervising
Coaching	Healing/treating	Observing	Teaching/training
Communicating	Hospitality	Operating equipment	Technical
Competing	Influencing	Organizing & implementing	
Computing	Interpersonal/social	Personal Service	Visual Arts
Constructing	Intervening	Personnel	Working with:
Consulting	Imagining/visualizing	Performing	people
Counseling	Importing/exporting	Persuading	animals
Creating	Instructional Design	Physical activity	data
Curriculum Development		Investigating	Planning
Decision-Making	Judging (moral)	Policy Development	Writing
Delegating	Leading	Politicking	OTHER SKILLS:
Designing	Using language	Presenting	Sewing
Developing	Managing	Promoting	Crafts
Economics	Manufacturing	Protecting/defending	Knitting
Editing	Marketing	Public Relations	Crocheting
Educating	Mathematics	Publishing	Building

Add any skills not listed that you enjoy using.

INVENTORY QUESTION #11:

The next Inventory Question covers every conceivable negative situation I could think of. What really "rattles your cage?" What makes you mad? What do you refuse to watch on television because of how it makes you feel? What rankles you about society?

Look at the Causes/Issues on the next page and choose three that really make you mad. You may feel strongly about all of them. That's fine, but narrow it down to three causes you would actually march for. Your choices tell you a bit about yourself.

The issues that make you react negatively are frequently those that are at odds with your strongly held values and beliefs. If your *issue* is missing, add it.

INVENTORY QUESTION #11: Check off those that you feel most strongly about?

CAUSES/ISSUES
(Circle three that most interest you)

Environmental pollution

Education reform

Health Care providers

Children: Abuse, neglect

The Homeless

The Justice System: laws and reform

Veterans: pensions, illnesses

Nutrition: sugar and fat debate; dieting

Politics: the fleecing of America

Youth: curfews, pregnancy

Business: taxes, laws, red tape

Churches: reform, separation

Spirituality: new age, propaganda?

Infants: regulations for protection

Child Care: mandatory training

Home Health Care: who pays

Tourism: protection of consumer, safety

Space Exploration: cost, safety, use

Animal Care: protection, training

Literacy: how it occurs, how to correct

Civil Rights Issues: dead or alive?

Fashion: real or unrealistic

Books: banned, controversial

Family Issues: training for parents

Media: irresponsibility

Elderly: nursing homes, medicare

The Poor: insurance; welfare

Immigration: laws, children born

Parks & Recreation: overuse

Substance Abusers: laws, crimes

Law: reform

Government: reform, deficit

Roads & Bridges: repairs, taxes

Non-profit Agencies: funding

Anti-Semitism

The Ill & Disabled: equal rights?

Child Protection: law reform

Justice: for the rich and powerful

Water: purity, safety, future

Defense: costs, necessity

Animal Rights: vivisection

Labor Relations: higher prices

Border Issues: discrimination

Sexuality Issues: who teaches

Art: first Amendment rights

Music: youth vs. adults

Movies: ratings war

Sports: becoming more violent

Computer Technology: way of future

Management: effective styles

Finance: rich vs. poor

Sincerity: importance of?

Community Development: malls vs. mom/pop

Research: morality issues

Women's Issues: who has right to body?

Broadcasting: responsibility

Human Relation Principles: value?

Design: regulations

Food: engineering, safety

Administration: equity, fairness

Construction: safety

Real Estate: laws, rights

Religion: war for God

Reproductive Issues: abortion

Biotech: going too far

Gardening: fertilizer safety

Civility: becoming rarer

Kindness: importance

EVERY ISSUE ON THIS LIST IS IMPORTANT; HOWEVER, YOU CAN ONLY SELECT THE THREE THAT YOU FEEL MOST STRONGLY ABOUT. LIST OTHER CAUSES AND/ OR ISSUES YOU HAVE AN INTEREST IN. *(Adapted from The Path by Laurie Beth Jones)*

INVENTORY QUESTION #12:

Your next Inventory Question is fun, and it will make you think. This exercise is another way of locating who you like to be around and what you like doing or being a part of.

The scenario is, you are moving out of your present home and are looking for a new condominium in which to live. You have to choose among eight locations, each filled with people of similar professions.

You may choose only one condominium where you would like to live. Look at the occupants you will be sharing the building with. Which group(s) do you most enjoy being with?

Make a second choice, again concentrating on the occupants in the building.

Enjoy choosing your condominium.

INVENTORY QUESTION #12: What are the occupations of the inhabitants in your favorite condo?

CONDOMINIUM CHOICES

Imagine yourself moving into a new condominium complex that leases space according to interests. The following condos are available. Where would you feel most comfortable? Because all of your socializing and dining will be with the group you choose, look carefully and see one which has people with whom you would be most compatible and would most enjoy being around on a regular basis.

CONDO #1: <u>Scientists (mind people)</u>: researchers, doctors, dentists, lawyers, judges.

CONDO #2: <u>Artists (free-spirited people)</u>: painters, designers, singers, dancers, comedians, actors, actresses.

CONDO #3: <u>Trainers (helpers)</u>: teachers, preachers, motivational speakers, writers, curriculum developers, presenters.

CONDO #4: <u>Leaders (persuaders)</u>: managers, negotiators, advertisers, supervisors, publishers, public relations, sales, advertisers

CONDO #5: <u>Economists (number people)</u>: engineers, clerical workers, computer programmers, bankers, mathematicians, marketers

CONDO #6: <u>Athletes (physical people)</u>: runners, basketball players, baseball players, football players, aerobic instructors, gymnasts, hikers, bikers, campers, coaches.

CONDO #7: <u>Naturalists (animal people)</u>: veterinarians, agriculturalists, nurturers, care givers, nurses, health aides, social services,

CONDO #8: <u>Builders (mechanical people)</u>: mechanics, inventors, repairers, technical services, constructing.

Which group of people would you most desire to spend time with?_____

LIST YOUR FAVORITE CHARACTERISTICS OF YOUR FAVORITE GROUP:

_____, _____, _____, _____

If, perchance, the condo of your choice were not available, which condo would be your second choice? _____

LIST FAVORITE CHARACTERISTICS OF SECOND GROUP:

_____, _____, _____, _____

The significance of your choices is something you cannot ignore. You chose the types of people you most enjoy being with. Because people tend to gravitate toward people like themselves, you may have found the type of career you are looking for in one or both of these groups. Maybe you can combine characteristics of both in order to discover your own passion.

INVENTORY QUESTION #13:

This completed page is of immense value to you. It is a compressed history of you, everything you can do, have experienced, know about, and recognize as a gift. Take your time and complete the exercise as thoroughly as you possibly can. This is one assignment for which getting help from friends and family is recommended.

Take an 8 1/2 x 11 sheet of paper and fold it in half--right side to left side. Then fold it the same way again so that you end up with four long, skinny columns. At the top of each column, write one of the following words: SKILLS, KNOWLEDGE, EXPERIENCE, TALENTS/GIFTS.

Skills: Take as much time as you need--maybe days--to fill in each column. It's easy to determine what skills you have: typing, wood working, skiing, cooking. Anything that is learnable is a skill, although it could also be a talent. I could learn to play the piano--a skill, but I may not have a talent for piano playing. List every skill you can think of, especially those you enjoy using. This may be your gift.

Knowledge: What do you enjoy reading and knowing a lot about: steam engine locomotives, dieting, global warming, computers, politics, space travel, rap, Hollywood gossip, raising dogs. List all of the subjects about which you are knowledgeable. Again, be sure you include those areas where you still pursue information. What books do you purchase? What do you Google?

Experience: What work have you done or what "hat" have you worn in life from as far back as you can remember? Paperboy, lawn mower, lawyer, secretary, salesperson, lifeguard, errand boy, sweeper, hockey player, baby sitter, caddie, cousin--the potential examples are endless. Write everything you can think of, no matter how long ago it occurred.

Talents/Gifts: This is the hardest column and is the one with which you may need help. What do you do naturally, without hesitation? What is "easy" for you? Family and friends may more easily be able to isolate what talents and gifts you have. Do you have a great sense of humor? Are you funny? Easy to talk to? A good presenter? Good teacher? Good friend? Good artist, dancer, singer? Good brother, sister? You may experience a feeling of embarrassment or humility when you relate what you believe your talent or gift is, and that is fine.

One gift you may have is ease in meeting people and making a good first impression. Someone who is nervous meeting people can recognize this as a talent or gift in someone else.

Look carefully at each column you've completed and circle your favorite thing, the thing that "calls" to you. Look at your four choices--one from each column--and see if you can come up with a way to combine the four and, as a result, make a difference in the lives of others.

To give you a personal example, my favorite *Skill* is teaching (and I believe it is also my talent). My favorite area of *Knowledge* is "people skills." In *Experience* is my work with "at risk" kids. And I believe my *Talent* is being able to understand, reach, and teach those I work with, especially "at risk" teens

The last Inventory Question is interesting because it is something you know, but may not know that you know. Think of all the encounters you have had with family and friends just this past week. Why did they come to you? For advice, to listen, to counsel? Divide the people in your life into different categories: friends, family, coworkers, children. Think of each one individually and remember what your last conversation with them was about. It may be "telling." It may be what you do naturally.

INVENTORY QUESTION #14:

What do people come to you for right now? It is advice on a school subject, sports, relationships, problems at school, any type of guidance or requested recommendations? How do people perceive you? What do they think are your strengths? For example, when my kids call home, they never ask me anything about insurance, cars, or money. On the other hand, they never ask their father about relationships and philosophical issues. What do people assume you know or can help them with?

INVENTORY QUESTION #15:

Complete the following sentence with as many completions as you can: "I am happiest when I am _____."

Many years ago, Werner Erhardt developed a seminar, EST (Erhardt Seminar Training), and one example he used stuck in my mind. He talked about someone whose passion was dancing. If you follow the **HAVE, DO, BE** pattern, you will **HAVE** to buy the tutu, **DO**-- take dancing lessons, or **BE** -- just dance. Keeping that example in mind, complete the following sentences:

I am happiest when I **have,**_____.(*Everything necessary to dance – music, costume, audience . . .*)

I am happiest when I **do** _____.(*Dance*)

I am happiest when I am (**being**) _____ .(*A dancer, feeling the music and moving with freedom and grace.*)

Try these exercises and keep in mind, your gift belongs to us! You can't give it away unless you are aware of it and use it. What greater satisfaction is there than doing what you love and making a difference in the world!

What do these two quotes from Werner Erhardt mean to you?

Create your future from your future not your past.

Ride the horse in the direction that it's going.

SECTION TWO

INVENTORY ANALYSIS

SESSION SIX

ANALYSIS OF PUZZLE PIECES

Analyze the influence of PEOPLE in your life from your responses to question #'s 1, 12, 14, Extra.

1. What do you like to hear said about you now?
12. What group of people did you choose in your condo?
14. What do people come to you for right now?
Extra. Whom do you admire in life and why do you admire them?

Analyze your answers for ACTIVITIES and PLACES: #'s 2, 4, 7, 8, 10, 12, 13, 15.

2. What childhood memory and achievement gives you the greatest pleasure to recall? Why?
4. Where do you most enjoy being?
7. What do you most enjoy reading about?
8. What do you most enjoy doing in your spare time?
10. What skills do you most enjoy using?
12. What are the occupations of the inhabitants in your favorite condo?
13. What is the commonality among your skills, experience, knowledge, and talents/gifts?
15. What activities are involved in your responses to "I am happiest when I am _____. (What do you most enjoy *doing*?)

Analyze the following questions about VALUES: #'s 1, 3, 5, 6, 11, 15.

1. What values are revealed in your responses to what you like to hear said about you?
3. What is so special about each memory and achievement you listed in Inventory Question #2?
5. What are your 3 most important internal values?
6. What are your 3 most important external values?
11. What causes/issues do you feel most strongly about?
15. What values emerge from your responses to "I am happiest when I am _____. (What do you most enjoy *being*?)

What are your TALENTS/GIFTS: #'s 9, 10, 13, 14.

9. What do you do easily, naturally?
10. What skills do you most enjoy using?
13. What talents/gifts/skills stand out or are repeated from this question?

14. What do people come to you for right now? It is advice on fitness, finances, relationships, problems at work, any type of advice, guidance, recommendations?

THE NEXT STEP:

Using what you have learned from this analysis, go to the Preliminary Summary and further reduce your responses to 10, then reduce your responses further to 3, and finally write how those three responses could lead you toward your passion or is your passion.

SESSION SEVEN

PRELIMINARY SUMMARY

1. Write the top three things you **most enjoy doing:**
(1)_____ (2) _____ (3) _____
2. Look at question No. 9. What do you **DO EFFORTLESSLY?** (4)_____
3. List your 3 **FAVORITE SAMPLE SKILLS: (5)** _____ **(6)**_____ **(7)** _____
4. Look at your condo choice. List your 3 **FAVORITE TYPES OF PEOPLE**:
(8) _____ (9) _____ (10)_____

From this list of 10 responses, narrow them down to your favorite three responses. These answers can come all from one question or from three questions. The combination is up to you.

1. _____
2. _____
3. _____

Look carefully at these three words, use your imagination, and come up with a money-making opportunity for your future. No answer is unreasonable. Have fun with this exercise. Let your imagination go wild. From your careful consideration of these three words, what is the unique career opportunity you would like to pursue? _____

Move on to Summary #I and complete that page for further clarification of your true interests. Then move on to Summary #II and enlist the aid of your friends.

Summary #1, which follows, is a further analysis of your questions. Answer these questions to the best of your ability. You want to employ as many methods as possible, from different angles or perspectives, in your quest to find what is most satisfying to you. Only you can do this analysis.

Preliminary Summary, Summary I and Summary II should be duplicated at least four times and given to four people who know you well. You will supply them with your Preliminary Summary and Summary #1 so they can study your answers and then come up with their own recommendations. **(THIS IS AN IMPORTANT STEP TO TAKE. Your friends know you and see you differently than you see yourself.)**

Frequently, finding what is special about yourself and what you most enjoy are more easily discerned by those closest to you.

When your family and friends have returned Summary #2 to you and you have had a chance to study all three summaries, you are then ready to work on the formation of your passion statement.

SESSION EIGHT

SUMMARY I
(From your Inventory Questions, complete the following questions.)

- Positive qualities you possess: _____
- Qualities you admire in people you admire: _____
- Places where you enjoy being: _____
- Most important External Values: _____
- Words to describe you personally: _____
- What you most enjoy reading about: _____
- Things you most enjoy doing: _____
- Things you most enjoy: _____
- What makes you feel good: _____
- What do you need to be happy?: _____
- How would you help people?: _____
- Favorite Causes/Issues: _____
- What gives you greatest pleasure?: _____

What career(s) would encompass the largest number of your responses?

_____

SUMMARY II

- Make four copies of the Preliminary Summary, Summary I and Summary II.
- Give these three Summary pages to four friends and ask them to complete the following:

DEAR FRIEND: From the Preliminary Summary & Summary #I sheets, what are your intuitive responses to the following questions?

- How do I most often describe myself?

_____

- What appears to be of greatest importance/interest to me?

_____

- What do I seem to enjoy most?

_____

- What do I seem to desire most in life?

  _____

- Whom do I seem to most enjoy associating with?

  _____

- What do you see as my natural abilities?

  _____

- What do you believe I most value?

  _____

- What do you feel I would most like to do?

  _____

JOB RECOMMENDATIONS

Using your own intuition, what do you see as my passion? All ideas welcomed!

_____

_____

_____

_____

_____

THANKS FOR YOUR HELP!!

SESSION NINE

PASSION STATEMENT

After you have received Summary II sheets from at least four people, sit down and study their responses. Have they seen anything in their words that you might have missed? What ideas do they suggest? No idea is crazy or dumb. In each idea there could be a germ of an idea ready to be released. Some of the craziest ideas sprout forth the best, most unusual ideas that may be just what you are looking for.

When you have fully completed the two steps, the time has come to put the pieces of the puzzle together and paint the picture of your passion.

- **STEP ONE**: List the most significant skills, in the form of **verbs (action words)**, which are found on your **Summary I and Summary II** sheets that were completed by your friends. Also look at the Sample Skills list for additional ideas.

_____

_____

Choose three of these action words from the above in verb form to complete the following sentence:

My passion is to:

(1) _____ **(2)** _____ **(3)** _____

(My personal response is "My passion is to research, write, and teach." I know that researching, writing, and teaching are three things that I will always gravitate to and always enjoy doing, even during my free time.)

- **STEP TWO:** With whom do you wish to use these skills? Check your answers to "People You Admire," "Causes/Issues," and "The Condominiums."

_____

_____

(My response to this step is "teens and young adults." I enjoy working with this population. I also enjoy working with senior citizens.)

- **STEP THREE:** What is the purpose of your **Steps One and Two**? What is the desired outcome of the use of your favorite skills?

_____ **(to do what?)**

To help you find the answer, check on your original answer sheet. What are your most important "Values"? Check "External and Internal Values," "Most Enjoy Reading," "Childhood Memories," "Places to Work," "Causes/Issues," "I Am Happiest When . . .," as well as any of the other responses you might have written.

(My response is "to find their 'specialness' and maximize their potential.")

- **STEP FOUR:** Combine all of the above steps into one statement. Make sure your statement is in present tense. It is now, not yesterday or tomorrow, but right now.

MY PASSION IS TO (SKILL) _____, (SKILL) _____
AND (SKILL) _____ (WITH WHOM?) _____
(FOR WHAT RESULT?) _____

(My single line statement of passion is "**My passion is to research, write, and teach teens and young adults how to maximize their potential in order to live a meaningful life.**")

- **STEP FIVE:** Write the single most important External Value you have listed previously and make sure it is not violated by your PASSION DISCOVERY.

EXTERNAL VALUE: _____

If this value is violated by your passion statement, you will invariably experience conflict within yourself. You may find that you have to make changes in some aspect of your statement. Your values are a "what is." They define who you are and can only change through your evolution in life, not through conscious deliberation.

- **STEP SIX:** The final question to ask yourself is **"What do I get out of this?**

It is imperative that you benefit from your passion; otherwise, it is not a true passion. Martyrdom is a state that is short-lived. You must genuinely benefit from what you choose to do. The awards may appear in the form of money and/or power, but the most satisfying reward, however, will come from waking up each morning **EXCITED** about the day, being **HAPPY** doing what you are doing, and having real **PURPOSE** in life. If _**EXCITED, HAPPY, AND PURPOSE**_ are not part of the benefit(s) you receive from your passion, then you may have to rethink your choices.

SECTION THREE

TOOLS FOR SUCCESS

SESSION TEN

TOOLS FOR SUCCESS

FOUR INTERNAL TOOLS

1. INTUITION

The search for your passion begins in your imagination. The search requires that you listen to your inner voice, your hunches, your intuition.

Intuition is a sense of knowing more than what is logical thought. This knowing has a logic of its own. Hunches are intuition. If you listen to your intuition, you will be inspired perhaps to take a new direction or stop your current pursuit. Being at the right place at the right time is also intuition.

More Thoughts on Intuition

1. **"The primary wisdom is intuition."** - Ralph Waldo Emerson
2. **"...[The pioneer scientist must have] a vivid intuitive imagination for new ideas that are not generated by deduction, but by artistically creative imagination."** - Max Planck
3. **"The term intuition does not denote something contrary to reason, but something outside of the province of reason."** - Carl Jung
4. **"My beliefs I test on my body, on my intuitional consciousness, and when I get a response there, then I accept."** – D. H. Lawrence
5. **"Most of us are living at the periphery of consciousness while intuition invites us into the center."** - Willia Harman
6. **"We are having this conversation about intuition because we all want to become real."** - Rob Rabin
7. **"When you let intuition have its way with you, you open up new levels of the world. Such opening-up is the most practical of all activities."** - Evelyn Underhill
8. **"Intuition is one of the most important abilities we can cultivate...It is becoming necessary for a comprehensive personal and global perspective."** - Jagdish Parikh
9. **"You feed your longing and desires, and they do the work. My whole life has been following my intuition and strange beckonings."** - David Whyte

You must constantly ask yourself what you love to do the most, then listen to your intuition for an answer. Your passion in life is about you, about your willingness to serve others while serving yourself. (Dr. Robert Anthony).

Keep in mind that some people find their way, seemingly more by intuition than anything else. An experience occurs, maybe by accident, and they relate to it. Something inside says, "Do it." Something clicks. A little light comes on. Listen for those inklings.

Listen to your inner voice. Relax during the day, close your eyes, clear your mind and listen. While you may not hear words, you may "feel" as if you should do something or respond in a certain way. Listen . . .

Personal Experience

Obviously, there is no one vocation or avocation that suits everyone. For example, I thought sales would be easy and enjoyable. Anyone can sell a product if there is a need for that product, or so I thought; so a few years ago I decided to sell for my husband in order to increase the volume of his computer supply business.

In addition to spending a week on the road with my husband, I studied the product line, ordered business cards, organized my briefcase, and set out on my first sales call.

I drove to an industrial park in a nearby town and chose a large, three-story office building as my first target. I walked into the building and was relieved to see that most of the offices had glass fronts that enabled me to see inside.

I approached the first office, noticed a very grumpy looking lady at the receptionist's desk and continued on my way. I certainly didn't want to bother her.

At the second office, the receptionist was on the phone--couldn't interrupt her, so I kept walking. At the third office, no one was at the desk--couldn't go in there. The last office, unfortunately, didn't have a glass front. I certainly couldn't enter unknown territory. That took care of the first floor.

Similar situations repeated themselves on the next two floors. I just could not make myself go into any office. I left the building feeling totally deflated.

The next day I tried again in a different location that housed individual office buildings. I fared little better. I was able to collect a few business cards but made no sales.

After numerous similar experiences, I decided to change my tactics. I chose the route of telemarketing.

When I phoned a man I had seen a few weeks before, he said in a disgusted voice, "You must be desperate." "Yes," I thought, "I am." Still no sales!

Thereafter I had the neatest, cleanest, most organized drawers, closets, and cabinets that I have ever had. I did anything to avoid placing the call. I could not make myself pick up the phone--after all, the junk drawer hadn't been cleaned out in 12 years.

I knew then that sales and marketing were definitely not my bailiwick. The point is, **how you feel makes a difference.** You should be able to look forward to what you are doing, not dread it as I did when I tried to sell. If it doesn't **FEEL** right, it probably isn't. Logic has nothing to do with it; intuition does.

To succeed at anything, you should truly love it and *feel* as if this is for you. Your ultimate goal should be to find what you love to do and become an expert at it. The process of learning will be more enjoyable than anything you have previously undertaken, because the learning will be directed toward what you want to learn about.

2.   **Thoughts**

Think of thoughts as "Things" in order to give substance to the concept of thought.

In all of the courses I teach, I stress two controllable areas of our lives we always have to be on top of:

(1) Thoughts
(2) Attitudes.

As you undertake the challenge of finding and profiting from your passion, I first and foremost want to emphasis how important your thoughts are in every aspect of your life, especially in your approach to this program.

As Norman Vincent Peale said, **"Change your thoughts and you change your world."** Of course, it sounds easier than it is. Our lives are not determined so much by our outward conditions and circumstances as it is by the way we perceive these conditions and circumstances. Read that sentence again and let it sink in.

Our world is basically what our thoughts make of it. Believe it or not, people have in their lives today exactly what they keep telling their mind they want.

Do you have what you want in your life? Your physical world today basically reflects all of the thinking you have or have not engaged in up to now. (Staples)

The poem "Thoughts Are Things" gives substance to the concept of thought.

THOUGHTS ARE THINGS

I hold it true that thoughts are things;
They're endowed with bodies and breath and wings:
And that we send them forth to fill
The world with good results, or ill.
That which we call our secret thought
Speeds forth to earth's remotest spot,
Leaving its blessings or its woes
Like tracks behind it as it goes.

We build our future, thought by thought,
For good or ill, yet know it not.
Yet so the universe was wrought.
Thought is another name for fate;
Choose then thy destiny and wait,
For love brings love and hate brings hate.

-Henry Van Dyke (*Think Like a Winner,* Staples)

In this course, thoughts/attitudes will make a difference between finding and pursuing your passion or maintaining the status quo.

Keep in mind a very important fact: **We become what we think about all day long**. Norman Vincent Peale stated, "You are not what you think you are, but what you think, you are." You have to really think about that.

Along the same line, Marcus Aurelious said, **"A man's life is what his thoughts make of it."**

Ralph Waldo Emerson said, **"A man is what he thinks about all day long."** Thoughts are very important, and you are the only one who can control them.

If you have negative thoughts, negative pictures in your mind, in all likelihood, you are headed in a negative direction with negative results.

On the other hand, positive thinking is productive and fulfilling. In *The Millionaire's Secrets*, Mark Fisher said, "Extraordinary people know that ideas are very real entities, that every idea we emit tends to concretize, attracting the people and circumstances that can help make it a reality. And it doesn't matter if the idea is positive or negative."

You can train yourself to think more positively by training yourself to choose what you pay attention to and what you say about it, both to yourself and others.

Imagine that you have the power to bring into being anything you desire merely by saying the words.
What would you say? How about
"I'm a very attractive person."
"I have a successful, lucrative career."
"I am thin, healthy, and fit."
"I always know what to say."
"People are attracted to my because of my wisdom."

Write what you would say if you wanted it to be true.

Your thoughts have energy. Make sure it is positive energy generated by positive thoughts.

"We know what we are but know not what we may be." - Shakespeare

Who chooses your thoughts? You do. Thoughts pop into your mind unsolicited, but you can change them, therefore, you have control of your thoughts. There is so much power in being able to internalize the fact that we are in charge of our thoughts, feelings, and reactions. We can't control what happens to us, but we are always in charge of our reactions to it.

> Example: Christopher Reeves, "Your attitude makes a difference, you have a choice. You can be passive and never leave your home and basically retire from life, or say 'I'm going to use everything I've got and try to do something.'"

Thoughts are more powerful than most people realize. In workshops, I demonstrate this fact by holding a string or thread between my pointer finger and thumb with a weight at the end of the string--a button, key, pendant, even a paper clip. I tell the audience to tell me which way I should THINK the object to move--left to right, up and down, clockwise circle, counterclockwise circle. I do not consciously move my finger, but I do think whatever direction I am told, and the object moves exactly as I tell it to. It is always amazing. 95% of the audience can do it as well. A very few cannot, and I don't know why--perhaps because they believe they can't.

If my thoughts can make my fingers move without conscious feeling or direction on my part, imagine what thoughts do to our minds and bodies every day.

Think about the quotes, "You are what you think about all day long," plus the others previously stated. There is truth in every one of them.

Thoughts determine belief, and belief is the motivating force that enables us to achieve our goals. Henry Ford said, **"If you think you can or you think you can't, you are right."** Believe you can discover your passion and earn money working at it, and it will be so.

The successful people throughout history have succeeded through their thinking. Hard work alone will not bring success. **Thought attracts that to which it is directed.**

An added caveat: **Thoughts with feeling are what causes belief.** You can think and think and think and have no reaction. However, **if you consciously think and feel, then you can manifest a belief of your choosing**.

Emotions are what prompt human beings to respond, to react. Words create emotion but will not create the same reaction in all people. What makes me angry can make my husband laugh and visa versa. Thoughts, using words that create emotion for you, are what you need to use in order to create the belief that you will be successful in whatever you choose to do.

To plant the beliefs we desire to have into our subconscious minds requires knowledge of the importance and methods of relaxation and visualization that is covered after "attitude" and more in-depth in Section Eight.

Another way to implant beliefs is through repetition. Years ago, Emile Coue, an 18th century physician told his patients to look in the mirror twice a day and repeat several times the phrase, "Each and every day I am getting better and better." He had remarkable results, so remarkable, in fact, that he was jailed for being a heretic.

Words actually have energy as shown by the string/pendant experience and Emile Coue's results.

Revisit the phrases list two pages ago, except now attach an emotion to each sentence and repeat each one that is meaningful to you again.

> I am a very attractive person.
> I have a successful, lucrative career.
> I am thin, healthy, and fit.
> I always know the right thing to say.
> People are attracted to me because of my wisdom.

Take some time and write down the beliefs you desire to have as part of you in each area of your life: socially, financially, physically, mentally, spiritually, etc. (Beliefs cause you to act and react, so choose carefully.)

Next, write the sentences you can repeat to bring these beliefs into being.

3. **Attitude**

Attitudes are thoughts, and attitudes rule our lives.

There is overwhelming evidence to support the premise that success results more from attitudes than any other single factor.

Attitudes are the result of decisions and choices you make on a daily basis.

Most great leaders have a positive attitude. Being positive is a choice.

Attitudes

The longer I live, the more I realize the importance
of choosing the right attitude in life.
Attitude is more important than facts.
It is more important than your past;
more important than your education or your financial situation;
more important than your circumstances, your successes, or your failures;
more important than what other people think or say or do.
It is more important than your appearance, your giftedness, or your skills.
It will make or break a company. It will cause a church to soar or sink.

It will make the difference between a happy home or a miserable home.
You have a choice each day regarding the attitude you will embrace.

Life is like a violin.
You can focus on the broken strings that dangle,
or you can play your life's melody on the one that remains.
You cannot change the years that have passed,
nor can you change the daily tick of the clock.
You cannot change the pace of your march toward your death.
You cannot change the decisions or the reactions of other people.
And you certainly cannot change the inevitable.
Those are strings that dangle!
What you can do is play on the one string that remains – your attitude.
I am convinced that life is 10 percent what happens to me
and 90 percent how I react to it.
The same is true for you.

Chuck Swindoll

Executive recruiters at Harvard University found in a study that 85% of everything a person accomplishes after university in the way of wealth, position, and status was the result of attitude; only 15% was the result of aptitude and abilities.

Similar research has found that there is no correlation between lifetime earnings and academic achievement.

Attitude accounts for a person's performance and progress at least 85% of the time.

If you choose a positive attitude, you tend to expect favorable outcomes.

Dennis Waitley in *The Psychology of Winning* says that successful people make a habit of manufacturing their own positive expectations in advance of the event. They have developed an attitude of positive self-expectancy, even though they cannot be certain things will always turn out exactly the way they want.

A positive attitude leads to positive, enthusiastic expectations that affect other people in a positive way and help bring about positive productive results. Positive attitudes are a powerful force that helps create its own reality. (Staples)

Samuel Johnson wrote, "He who has so little knowledge of human nature as to seek happiness by changing anything but his own disposition (attitude) will waste his life in fruitless efforts and multiply the griefs which he proposes to remove."

Now that the importance of thoughts (attitudes) in our lives has been established, let's look to the future and see what lies ahead. Remember, "You are not what you think you are, but what you think, you are." -Norman Vincent Peale

4. Relaxation and Visualization

Train yourself to relax and visualize yourself doing what you want to do. Meditate on the good things currently in your life.

Relaxation is a simple process. Sit in a chair or lie on the floor. Take a few deep breaths, exhale slowly, and allow all of the tension to flow out of your body. Feel your body become loose and limp.

Visualize a soft, internal light shining on the top of your head, relaxing all of the muscles of your scalp; see the light move down to your forehead, your cheeks, your chin, erasing all the worry, all the tension from your face.

Feel your face become loose and limp and your jaw hang loose. Feel the warmth and relax the muscles in your neck, your shoulders, both arms, torso, buttocks, thighs, calves, feet, and toes.

Once all of the muscles in your body are relaxed, breathe in, then out, in, then out, allowing your mind to relax and concentrate only on your breath.

Remain in this relaxed position for a ten to fifteen minutes, then visualize on the blank screen of your mind, exactly what you would like to see yourself doing, exactly what gives you the greatest pleasure.

Who's involved? Where are you? What is the temperature? Try to notice details. They may change daily, and that's okay.

When your mind is relaxed, ideas flow more readily. Have you ever had the experience of going to bed after an argument with someone, and once your head hits the pillow, you think of the greatest things you should have said? Or you have the greatest opening for the letter you have put off writing?

The reason the ideas come now or in the shower or when you are driving is because that is when your mind is most relaxed and your brain waves have slowed down. That is when your mind can more readily access the right part of your brain where the creativity lies.

Relaxation has numerous physical benefits--lowered blood pressure being one of them--but the reason I emphasize it here is because relaxation also makes your mind work better when going through the various exercises.

I have a simple secret. I use a timer and set it to ring every two hours. It keeps me in the present, reminds me to take deep breaths, inhaling health and wealth, exhaling judgment and negativity.

Of the numerous personal examples of the value of relaxation and visualization I've experienced, one in particular stands out--perhaps because it was the first result I was consciously aware of.

In the early 70's Joe Karbo wrote a book, *The Lazy Man's Way to Riches*, which he advertised in *Parade Magazine*. He offered a money-back guarantee and went on to say the book cost him only $.50 a copy, and he was selling it for $10. I ordered a copy, and I wasn't disappointed. The book was worth every penny.

In his book, Karbo's recommendation is to list everything you want in life and then narrow your list to the most important thing you desire, e.g., *a house in a nice neighborhood*. Concentrate (e.g., relax and visualize) on this in the morning and in the evening.

After I did this for six months, a friend called, asking me if we wanted to buy her parent's house, which is located in a beautiful town with excellent schools. Napoleon Hill said, "**Whatever your mind can conceive and believe, it can achieve.**"

In spite of my six months of focusing on a house in a nice neighborhood, I wasn't initially interested because we had just purchased new carpeting and storm windows for our current home. Because she is such a close friend, we decided to look at the house. WOW! Viola, it was so familiar looking. It was close to the vague picture of a house I had been concentrating on and visualizing for months. Needless to say, we bought the house and have lived in it now for over 40 years. Coincidence???

I could tell you many incidents where I consciously concentrated on something, which then came true. That's for another course someday.

Key Point: If you follow the schedule and use the internal and external tools recommended, you will not only discover your passion but also profit from it. (More detailed information on this topic is found in Session 30, "Six Steps to Success.")

SESSION ELEVEN

THREE EXTERNAL TOOLS

HELPFUL, INVALUABLE HABITS TO DEVELOP: I strongly recommend the three following activities. These three tools are worth incorporating into your daily routine, even if you weren't looking to find your passion. These tools are particularly valuable for the process of creating the life you desire.

1. **Start keeping a journal**

In your journal write ideas you get at odd moments. Include your reactions to a movie, a book, a letter, a conversation--anything that is meaningful to you. Record what you are grateful for each day, especially if you are having trouble feeling positive.

Include your reactions to the various exercises as you complete them in this program. And, most important, write down your plans as they begin to form in your mind.

Start keeping track of what you like about each segment of the day. Are you an early riser? Do you like to work late? Are there certain types of people who motivate you, make you feel good about yourself? Analyze them. Analyze why you react to them as you do.

Eventually your journal will contain a myriad of events--information, which, as you reread, may begin to form a pattern. Certain ideas, topics, people keep reoccurring. All of that is significant.

Make it a point to write every day, even if only for a few minutes. Your journal is a reminder that you are on the path toward your passion. It is a visual reminder to keep you on target, to remind you to stay focused.

I highly recommend Julia Cameron's book, *The Artist's Way*. In it, the author suggests you write three pages each a.m. She calls them the *morning pages*. I faithfully did this at 5:30 a.m. (often with only one eye open), and from those *morning pages* came many of the programs I've developed over the years. Early a.m. is good because the little censor in your brain is still asleep. You know the one I'm talking about, the one who whispers in your ear, "That's stupid!" "Who cares?" "Who do you think you are?" and other uninspiring thoughts.

Later I'll discuss compiling what you learn about yourself into a 16-page booklet, so others can learn from you and your experiences. An example is my booklet *134 Tips for Teachers* that contains the basics of my philosophy which is practiced in all of my courses (this is covered in the Marketing Section).

2. Self Coaching

First, if you do not have a firm grasp on your passion, ask yourself, "What would my passion be if I did know?"

Write down whatever comes to your mind. Make it up, if necessary.

Second, if you were at a party and someone asked you what you do, what would you **LIKE** to be able to answer?

Those two questions are forms of self coaching or internal dialogue. You may be surprised at what responses you get from yourself.

On a sheet of paper, start your dialogue. On one line, **write "ME" and ask the question you want your mind to answer**, e.g., "What is my passion?"

On a separate line, **write "COACH" and have your internal coach respond**, for example, "It's obvious what your passion is. You are always giving people advice, so pick an area where you can do this and earn money."

> **"ME:"** "How can I do that?"

> **"COACH:"** "Simple, brainstorm every occupation you can think of where you can give advice to people, starting with teaching, guidance, coach . . ."

AND so forth, until you can think of no more questions.

For added help, pick up any career manual in your local book store, and you will see hundreds of types of jobs listed. Each has many facets, e.g., accountant--requires knowledge, skill, dealing with people, running a business, advertising, answering phones, filing, etc. Maybe you don't like the accounting part, but do like the organizational part.

Keep in mind, you are looking for something you love doing. It does not have to be a specific career; it could be something within a career.

It is amazing the answers your own brain will give you. One client sent me a copy of what she found out about herself, which she regarded as quite profound and something she was not consciously aware of. Her journal reads as follows:

> *ME: Hello Coach. I am 50 years old and have been dieting unsuccessfully for 39 years-- incredible! What is holding me back from eating healthful foods and exercising?*

> *COACH: My dear, I recognize how hard you have tried, how many books you have read, how much money you have spent, and how persistent you've been. Part of what you have to understand is that sweet foods equate to love and warmth from your childhood. Your*

mother was not someone who hugged you or told you she loved you She showed her love through the goodies she made you.

Not exercising is your dislike of sweating, which is no doubt due to your belief that you always have to look perfect--your hair has to always look good, you must be neat, you must have your makeup on perfectly.

Again, going back to your childhood, you believed your acceptance was based on how you looked.

ME: *Wow! I guess I knew this but now 'What can I do to undo my past associations?' is the question I need answered.*

COACH: *You have to "get" that people like you as you are. You have a fear of people talking about you--your weight, your hair, your clothes--why? It doesn't matter. Keep that in mind--it doesn't matter!*

You already have the answers inside you.

Try accessing your own brain. All the answers are there. Just ask!

3. **Mindmapping Exercise**

Mindmapping is a form of brainstorming on paper. If you would like more information on this subject, two experts in the field are Michael Gelb and Tony Buzan. Gelb has a tape series entitled *MindMapping*, and Tony Buzan, a brain expert, has a book by the same name.

MINDMAPPING EXERCISE TO HELP CLARIFY YOUR PASSION:

SITUATION:

You have five years before the end of the world. You want to live fully, reach your goals, and fulfill your dreams. This exercise will help you determine how you will spend these years.

When I taught high school English, my students had to write research papers on some aspect of British literature. To help them narrow their topics, I would have them do a mindmap.

In the center of their paper, I would have them write and circle "Elizabethan England." Drawing lines from the circle, the kids would brainstorm ideas such as "politics," "religion," "economics," "theater," etc. They would circle this set of words and continue brainstorming. For example, if they chose "theater," they would draw lines for "actors," "costumes," "playwrights," etc. As the topic narrowed, they could then opt to research that subject.

You can do the same type of brainstorming for ideas for your passion, using what you have already learned about yourself from your Inventory Questions.

STEP ONE:

In the center of a large sheet of paper, put the word **"PASSION"** directly in the middle of the page and circle it.

Draw lines going outward from the circle, then, at the end of each line, write whatever pops into your mind, e.g., "teaching," "writing," "building," "organizing," "helping," "caring for people, animals, flowers, etc." Write as fast as you can. Using your responses to the word "passion" as a checklist, write everything (from that list) you would be interested in doing in the next five years, and mindmap each of those topics.

Each word will be at the end of a line drawn from your center circle. Draw a circle around each word you write, and continue outward from that circle if more ideas come, e.g., from our "PASSION circle" could be the words "helping others."

Circle those words and draw more lines from that, answering "How you are going to help others." Continue until you can think of nothing else.

Keep mapping until the circled words are clarified. Are they supportive or in conflict? Make separate maps on each major area.

Ask why this is important to you. How do these goals reflect your life purpose?

STEP TWO:

Take your secondary words (those that emanated from your first word, "PASSION" and on a separate page, make a list, leaving room between your major words.

Continue brainstorming ideas, no matter how silly they may seem to you. (Remember, every now and then a germ of an idea is embedded in a seemingly inane thought or word.)

Continue until you have explored all of your words. Does anything pop out at you? Do you see a relationship between words? Is there a recurring theme?

For example, if WRITING were your passion, put that word in the center of your paper. Draw lines from it such as "FICTION," "NONFICTION," then draw lines from one of these, example from "NONFICTION," draw lines for "PETS," "BEAUTY," "PERSONAL DEVELOPMENT," "BASEBALL," "HOW TO . . ." until you have exhausted the topics which are of interest to you. Draw more lines from one of these topics until you narrow your topic as much as you can.

My passions are researching, teaching, and writing. I combined these into WRITING/TEACHING which implies using research but not as a separate entity.

From WRITING/TEACHING, I draw more lines which included topics: DISCOVER YOUR PASSION, PERSONAL DEVELOPMENT, MIND TECHNIQUES, HYPNOSIS,

RELAXATION--all topics that I'm interested in and would enjoy researching, teaching, and writing about.

From those topics I drew lines to include my potential audience: HIGH SCHOOL STUDENTS/ COLLEGE STUDENTS, RETIREES, DISSATISFIED EMPLOYEES.

From the people, I drew lines to indicate how I'd reach different groups: e-zines, articles, talks, seminars, workshops.

The lines can continue outward as more ideas spring into your mind. You are creating your own brainstorming session. Each line stimulates another idea. An added bonus is it's fun to do.

Mindmaps are useful for planning vacations, planning social events, expressing thoughts in writing, determining plot, characters, scenes, finding solutions to problems, plus much more.

Go for quantity, not quality. Keep a sense of humor, suspend your judgment, just keep writing and have fun!

Before you begin your next session, challenge yourself to have a PASSION to work with. It may change in a week, month, year. That's okay. Each adventure is a lesson learned.

Mindmapping can be used for a variety of projects. I use one when I am beginning a new book or course. For me, it is easier than outlining, which I hated to do in school.

On my wall, I have a flip chart sheet which has "coachability" (my website name) in the center with spikes drawn out to include all the areas that my site covers. For example, "speaking" is one course I teach and write about. From "speaking" I have written "classes," "teleclasses," "seminars," "books," "e-books." Each of those is a potential profit center for me. Seeing them on a daily basis is like having a motivational chart in front of me. **Try it! I believe you will enjoy the exercise.**

SESSION TWELVE

<u>REVIEW</u>

1. How did you react to your self coaching? What did you learn about yourself?

2. What did you learn from your mindmapping?

3. What did your summaries reveal about you?

4. SUMMARY II - What were you surprised to learn from your friend's/family's input?.

NOW, HOW CAN YOU MAKE MONEY FROM YOUR PASSION???

SECTION FOUR

FIND YOUR BUSINESS

DISCLAIMER

The concepts in Sections Four and Five regarding setting up an online or offline business are included to encourage you to keep your mind open for the time in your future when you may want to consider these possibilities.

Please know that you are not expected to complete Sections Four and Five.

Finding a business related to your passion and marketing principles are included to give you an idea of how to proceed with building that business when the you reach that point in your life.

Another avenue to consider is how to earn income for necessities unrelated to a passion. Chris Guillebeau, author of numerous books, including *The Money Tree* and *Side Hustle, from idea to income in 27 days* has over a thousand podcast interviews with people who started a side hustle to earn money, and many times that hustle turned into a passion.

Examples:

- Man earns $7,000 a month writing fish tank reviews,
- Craigslist wedding photographer,
- "Airbnb for dogs,"
- Guitar teacher sells lessons on Craigslist and Makes $80/hour,
- Visit to the ballpark inspires a unique fashion item,
- Facebook photo leads to Today Show appearance,
- Man learns to make and sell candles by watching YouTube,
- Student tutors friends in math,
- Worm composting empire started by student,
- College student earns $20,000 a month cleaning houses,
- iPhone photo leads to series of on-line courses,
- College buddies create $15,000 bow-tie hustle.

These ideas are just a few ideas to earn extra money. In many instances, the hustle idea turned into a passion.

What do you know right now that could benefit others, and how could you charge for your knowledge?

SESSION THIRTEEN

PROFIT CENTERS

First, think about the types (other than monetary) of profits people reap who practice their passion: mental, physical, spiritual, social.

- **MENTAL:** Working your passion means a stimulated, excited, mind that works faster, better, more frequently.

LIST AT LEAST THREE OTHER MENTAL BENEFITS YOU WOULD EXPERIENCE.

1.

2.

3.

- **PHYSICAL**: Research shows that frowning, the result of a poor mental attitude, has been proven to raise the level of adrenaline and lower the level of serotonin, thus producing all the physical systems of fear (elevated pulse, shallow breathing, slowed digestion, etc.)

When you feel good about what you are doing, you tend to stand straighter, allowing more blood to get to the brain. You tend to smile more.

WITH a conscious effort to the contrary, your facial expression, more than any other physical attribute, is a reflection of your emotional state.

LIST AT LEAST THREE PHYSICAL BENEFITS YOU WOULD EXPERIENCE, IF YOU FOLLOWED YOUR PASSION.

1.

2.

3.

- **SPIRITUAL:** Working your passion allows you to be in touch with your spiritual side. You are making a difference in the world.

LIST AT LEAST THREE SPIRITUAL BENEFITS YOU WOULD EXPERIENCE, IF YOU FOLLOWED YOUR PASSION.

1.

2.

3.

- **SOCIAL:** People gravitate to happy people, people who smile, people who are enthusiastic--charismatic.

LIST AT LEAST THREE SOCIAL BENEFITS YOU WOULD EXPERIENCE, IF YOU FOLLOWED YOUR PASSION.

1.

2.

3.

We recognize the value of **mental, physical, spiritual, social profit centers,** now let's move on to monetary or profit centers for your passion.

Hopefully, you have received your Summary sheets back from your friends and are clear on your passion--or at least have a direction to take.

YOU NOW HAVE YOUR PASSION, SO "HOW CAN YOU EARN MONEY FROM DOING WHAT YOU LOVE?"

- **Be--Do—Have** Previously I mentioned the EST (Erhardt Seminar Training) seminar in the early 80's, I learned that we sometimes do things backwards. We first have to **have,** e.g., a dancer buys a tutu and ballet slippers, then she **does,** which means she takes ballet lessons, then she can **be.** Why not do it the other way around? (See Inventory Question #15)

BE YOUR PASSION, then do it, and you'll have it.

Shakespeare said, "Assume a virtue if you have it not." Weight Watchers says, "Fake it until you make it." **Pretend to be and you will become.**

Each year at the university my son attended, there was be a hypnotist who would bring the shyest student on stage, whisper in the young man's ear, giving him directions to merely stand tall, shoulders back, head high and said loudly, "Welcome to our show." The audience was astounded. They believed the student was hypnotized. He wasn't. He merely assumed the posture of being confident and impressed the audience by the apparent change in his personality, e.g. fake it until you make it.

The point is, when you are perceived in a certain way, you tend to attract people who treat you accordingly.

Assuming you desire to make money, then someone will be paying you in some way. Let's look at few options.

SESSION FOURTEEN

Time to think about the future: Do you think you want an Off-line or an On-line business?

OFF-LINE BUSINESS MARKETING
(Selling a product or service)

MUST DO'S:

- **The objective of any business is "getting customers."** You could have the greatest product on the market, but if people don't come, they can't buy.

  - **Bring traffic to the store by**

    - holding sales.
    - giving something (coupon, free reports, samples) to everyone.
    - holding events--signings, parties, holiday themes, demonstrations.
    - advertising in the local papers.
    - advertising on local cable station. 30 second spots on CNN and ESPA are not that expensive. There is also Nick, TNN, BET, and V-1 to consider. These are definitely worth looking into.
    - writing articles. Eardly T. Peterson, a vacuum retailer in our town, has developed the reputation of being a true professional. Whenever a new product comes on the market, the owner's son, Keith, is trained and then writes an article about the training and the benefits customers will experience by buying this new product. He has expanded his product line to include sewing machines and possesses the expertise to convince anyone interested in sewing to buy from him.
    - print flyers on brightly colored paper and distribute them on public bulletin boards (grocery stores convenience stores, colleges & universities, health clubs, libraries, community centers, etc.).
    - NETWORK: Join Chambers of Commerce, Conferences, parties, etc., Professional Groups, etc.

  - **Join Networking Groups**

    - Networking Groups, e.g., BNI, Le Tip
    - Speak to groups: (Rotary, AAUP, Alumni groups, American Business Women Assoc., Board of Realtors, Business and Professional Women's Clubs, Political Clubs, Educational Organizations, Elks, Kiwanis, Libraries, Lions, Moose, Optimists, PTA's, Religious Groups, Senior Citizen Groups, Singles Clubs, etc.)

- **Offline Promotions**

  - Printed materials: business cars, brochures, postcards, price lists, etc.
  - Referrals
  - Writing: articles, newsletters, columns
  - Mailings
  - Direct Mail (Google "Direct Mail")
  - Telemarketing (scripts needed)
  - Proposals

ON-LINE BUSINESS MARKETING

Consider the possibility of selling knowledge related to your passion--writing a column, e-zine, or book; speaking/work-shops/seminars/teaching (Go back to your question responses for ideas).

- If you can talk, you can write. The point is to transfer your knowledge, not dazzle people with fancy words. You can always get an editor who can correct your grammar. Google: "How to Write an e-Book." For editorial services, go to upwork.com or fiverr.com.
- What are your interests? Little League, golf, fishing, raising children, throwing parties, decorating, cooking, packing, traveling, etc.
- What kinds of knowledge could you sell? Look at your answers to question #14 in your packet? What do people come to you for? You may have knowledge that that you take for granted, but that other people would pay to receive. Think about a particular skill you have—tennis, baseball, calculus, geometry, anything you ave mastered,
- Years ago, when I started working on the internet, I would have paid for an e-book on the subject of how to succeed on the internet. Now you can Google how to do almost anything. Other e-books I would have been interested in are self-publishing or raising an older adopted dog or training compassion dogs or meditation or parenting skills or spirituality or simplicity, plus many more. Do you have knowledge in any of these areas? If you do, write an article, then two or more. If you do write articles they become chapters, which is the beginning of a book.

What would you like to know more about? Maybe you can learn and then help others

- What do you know that others don't?
- What do you feel strongly about--look at list of issues?
- Your passion could be foisted on you due to a circumstance or an unexpected event, as mentioned previously-- MADD, Adam's father on America's Most Wanted, Christopher Reeves, etc.

- **LIST AT LEAST THREE IDEAS OR SPECIAL AREA OF KNOWLEDGE YOU COULD SELL: (Go to http://www.tipsbooklets.com for ideas about topics people are writing about and selling.)**

  1.

  2.

  3.

SESSION FIFTEEN

Consider the possibility of selling services related to your passion--coaching, teaching, consulting, seminar training, etc.

- Affiliates: There are over **over 70 million** affiliated programs in the google.com directory. Sample affiliates are Amazon.com, coachville.com, AdSense and so many more. You could set up an entire business just selling affiliate merchandise. There is considerable information available about affiliates. Did you know that if you buy one thing from me, perhaps a book, on amazon, I will get a commission on everything else you buy on amazon that day!

ASSIGNMENT:

> Go to www.google.com and type in AFFILIATES. The second item that came up when I typed AFFILIATES was "A free site that reveals the programs, tools and techniques which elite **affiliates** use to EARN THOUSANDS OF DOLLARS online. Check out what is available.

- Affiliates: For me, the most logical affiliate is amazon.com.

LIST THREE TYPES OF AFFILIATES YOU MIGHT WANT TO BECOME INVOLVED WITH:

1.

2.

3.

- **Teaching** is the best way to learn something you really desire to know. When I began teaching, I did not know grammar that well. I did the exercises with the kids, but it was through teaching grammar that I mastered it. Years ago I taught the Wang word processor. My training was skimpy at best, so I stood behind a monitor and learned as I taught. CAN YOU RELATE TO THIS?

Teaching does not have to be in schools that require teacher certification. Many private schools will accept the alternate route for teachers who have knowledge in the subject area that the school needs.

Adult schools require people who know their subjects, but they do not require a degree to teach their specialty. In our local adult school, the one course that is sold out every semester is the one taught by a landscaper. He became successful doing what he loves and now shares his knowledge with others. I'm sure his classes generate increased business for him.

Seminar leaders deliver information, but may not have had formal education training. What they do have is knowledge related to the subject on which they are speaking.

LIST THREE SUBJECTS YOU WOULD WANT TO TEACH:

1

2.

3.

Coaching is a wonderful profession for people with different areas of expertise. Coachville.com makes learning to coach people in your area of interests easy to learn. Check out Jeff Walker affiliates and watch his videos,

How often have you been asked for advice, been consulted on your favorite pastime without compensation? Who asks you?

The way I became involved with teaching *Discover Your Passion, an Intuitive Search to Find Your Purpose in Life* was as a result of so many people asking me for help, once they knew I had looked into the subject. Initially I taught *Discover Your Passion* at adult schools, but so many friends could not attend the class, yet they wanted the information. That's how I decided to write the book. It was written from my lesson plans that I had constantly updated over the years of teaching the course.

As the requests expanded beyond finding one's passion, I did further research, which led to the development of this book, *Discover Your Passion for Teens*. Teaching led me to write the book.

By responding to people who ask you questions, your ideas become clarified.

Teaching also led me to coaching people one-on-one or through online classes on exploring their passion.

LIST THREE TYPES OF PEOPLE OR SITUATIONS YOU WOULD WANT TO COACH:
(corporate coach, personal development coach, artistic coach, small business coach, ADD, relationship coach, sports coach, and many other niche areas).

1

2.

3.

Gail A. Cassidy

SESSION SIXTEEN

Consider the possibility of selling products related to your passion. Products could include software, a training program, affiliate products, DVD's, CD's, tips booklets ...

Remember, people don't make logical decisions to buy. In most cases, they make emotional decisions, but they need to have logic behind them to explain why they bought what they did. There is a need to combine emotion and logic.

Product Ideas: the best mousetrap, sleeves to protect your arms from being splattered, post-it notes with sayings, jelly, tea, software, whatever you can think of that relates to your passion. Have you ever improvised something that you could sell to others?

My friend Lorna worked for a medical supply company, but she loves jewelry. She left her company, enrolled in the Gemology Institute in New York, graduated at the top of her class, got a job at Tiffany's, took up golf, had a child and decided to stay home. Now she is designing upscale jewelry for golfers. She has discovered and is profiting from her passion.

- Hold free classes online or in person for those who might be interested in a product or service you have to sell. Get yourself known in your field.

LIST THREE TYPES OF PRODUCTS YOU WOULD WANT TO SELL:

1.

2.

3.

SESSION SEVENTEEN

Decide on your profit center

- What ideas come into your mind when you think about a "profit center?" Do you want an on-line business or an off-line business such as a retail business, a non-profit experience, a research project, a motivational speaker-type job, a medical-type job, engineering project, what . . .?
- What questions do you need answered?
- Who can help you?

I read a delightful book entitled *Find Your Passion*. The book relates an experience of a young boy who has a Malaysian father and an American mother. They lived in Massachusetts. While the boy was still young, his mother died of cancer. One day the boy came home and his father was all packed to go back to Malaysia. He said he always wanted to design shirts and manufacture them, so together they moved.

Years later the young boy asked his sweetheart to marry him. She wrote him a note, telling him she would marry him when he found his passion in life. She could see he hated working in his father's factory.

He went to America and stayed in a hotel where there happened to be a convention of retailers. He saw one table displaying beautiful men's shirts. Because his father did not like to market, his business was about to fail. The young man thought that perhaps his father could manufacture the beautiful shirts he saw displayed at the convention less expensively in his county.

He contacted the president of the company, and after a few obstacles, got the contract to manufacture the shirts and was quite excited. He had found his passion by becoming aware of the parts of his life that he already knew and liked. He hated the factory; he loved the art of deal making

This is a simple story, but it makes a point: find the aspect of what you are already doing or have done that you love doing and expand on it.

SECTION FIVE

MARKETING

(The science of encouraging people to buy)

These are effective principles for marketing a product or service. It's good to have this background information as you decide what you want to do in life.

SESSION EIGHTEEN

GENERAL PRINCIPLES:

1. **Find your audience.** (My primary audiences are educators.) The message for each audience is different. Having a single focus is the easiest way to be successful. You can then target all of your energies to that one group. For example, the web site, http://www.stopyourdivorce.com, is obviously targeted for one audience. The author has made a lot of money on this one e-book.

2. **Find out what they want**

Write a single statement of who your target audience is, what their needs are, and what motivates them. Your target audience is the people who would be interested in what you are selling.

Have a file folder for each group. On the outside of the folder list your products. On the inside, write statements for each product. (This is an exercise that can take hours and days. Run your material by a friend to see how she reacts.)

When you have your products and your audiences clearly in mind, you still need to find the audience's needs and motivators (what's in it for them?) When you are clear about their needs and motivators, you then tailor your products to address those needs--a great advantage when you have e-books.

3. **Answer their needs**

- Have a very clear message. "You can improve your golf swing."
- Define what each group wants, what motivates them. "You can eliminate colds."
- Be clear about the benefits for each group. "You will feel calm and relaxed,"
- Create a mental picture, "You can build inner strength--inner wealth--and unshakable confidence with my speaking and imaging course."

4. **Isolate the benefits for your target audience.** (How will your service or product eliminate their pain or discomfort?)

In Tony Robbin's book, *Unlimited Power*, he explains how everyone gravitates toward pleasure and avoids pain. Direct your target audience toward pleasure and make it reachable for them.

5. **Create the message that will hook the reader**

- Your message must answer **"What's in it for me?"**
- Your message must contain an emotion. Again, see http://www.stopyourdivorce.com for an example of a good sales letter.

6. **State your credentials**

If I am going fishing in Alaska and am looking for a guide, I don't care if the guide graduated with an MBA from Harvard. I do care that he has experience fishing in Alaska.

- Give testimonials.

Go to http://www.coachability.com/bookstore/books/testimonials/testimonials.html for examples of testimonials. An effective way to use testimonials is to weave them throughout your sales letter so your potential client is constantly exposed to the effectiveness of your product or service.

7. **20% of your marketing ideas will produce 80% of your results** (Pareto Principle).

8. **Build a Professional Success Team.**

Below is a blank list similar to those used by local networking group, such as BNI, (Business Networking International), of all the different occupations available. Add to it by going through the yellow pages. Fill in each occupation with someone you know or know of, contact that person and ask him if you could recommend him to your new customers as you set up your business. This is a mutually beneficial undertaking. They become aware of what you do and can then recommend you to someone who needs your services, and you can recommend them under the same circumstances.

PERSONAL PROSPECT LIST

Even if you are in high school or college, start making as many contacts as you can. You never know when they can be of help to you or you to them. Networking is a key ingredient in getting the job you most desire or in developing a customer base. Cross out those occupations that you know will never be of interest to you as a prospective employer or customer.

OCCUPATION	NAME	ADDRESS	PHONE #
Accountant			
Advertising agency			
Air conditioning			
Answering Service			
Appliance Repairs			
Appliance Sales			
Architect			
Art Dealer			
Artist			
Auctioneer			
Auto Body Repair			
Auto Mechanic			
Auto Sales			
Banker			
Barber			
Bookkeeping			
Book Shops			
Builder			
Business Broker			
Cabinet Maker			
Carpenter			
Carpet Cleaner			
Caterer			
Cellular Phones			
Chiropractor			
Clothing Sales			
Coach - Business			
Computer Hardware			
Computer Repair			
Computer Sales			
Computer Software			
Dentist			

Doctor _____

Dry Cleaners _____

Electrician _____

Employment Agency _____

Event Planner _____

Fence Contractor _____

Financial Advisor _____

Florist _____

Formal Wear _____

Funeral Director _____

GenMaintenance _____

Graphic Design _____

Hair Stylist _____

Hardware Contractor _____

Internet Services _____

Insurance _____

Interior Design _____

Jeweler _____

Landscaper _____

Lawyer _____

Lighting Fixtures _____

Locksmith _____

Magician _____

Management Consultant _____

Manicurist _____

Marketing Consultant _____

Mortgage Banker _____

Mortgage Broker _____

Newspaper Advertising _____

Nursery _____

Office Furniture _____

Office Supplies _____

Optometrist _____

Organizer _____

Orthodontist _____

Osteopath _____

Parties/Entertainment _____

Pest Control _____

Pharmacy _____

Photographer _____

Plumber _____

Printer _____

Psychologist _____

Public Relations _____

Real Estate _____

Radio Advertising _____

Secretarial Services _____

Signs _____

Solar Energy _____

Security Systems _____

Sound Systems _____

Sporting goods _____

Stockbroker _____

Surveyor _____

Swimming Pools _____

Therapist _____

Translator _____

Travel Agent _____

Trophies _____

TV Advertising _____

TV Repair _____

Tire Dealer _____

Upholsterer _____

Vending Service _____

Veterinarian _____

Web Page Design _____

Window Treatments _____

Word Processing _____

OTHER

_____

_____

_____

Continue to work on building and updating your list, and keep in touch with those who could be of value to your potential business.

Again we are talking about the future, so once you have names **you would like to work with or who could be of value to you**, follow up with a letter telling each person on your list what you do and how they could help you in the same way, by recommending you.

Update monthly. If you are working with others, send out a letter to your team to let them know what you are doing. Make sure they know you will recommend them also.

Again, your primary objective is to get your name out there and be recognizable.

SESSION NINETEEN

To get started on what you see as a potential career, develop a Tips booklet on a product or service in your profit center. (See your mindmap to locate all of your areas of interest.) Go to http://www.tipsbooklets.com for ideas.

Work on establishing your brand. My brand is helping people maximize their potential. My products **VALIDATE** (*The Validating Mentor*), **DIRECT** (*Profit From Your Passion*), *and* **POLISH** (*You Cannot Not Communicate*). All of my courses are geared to that result. I'm the "*passion lady.*"

What distinguishes you from others? Your product, service, or knowledge must center on helping others solve a problem in some way. The idea is to be the best that you can be in your area of expertise and money will follow.

SPECIFICALLY:

1. List your audience(s).
2. List as many benefits as you can for each product, service, or knowledge that you are offering.
3. Write about what the ultimate advantage of your service is?
4. Write everything you know about your subject, e.g., the features.
5. Write as if this will be an instruction manual for those employed by you. This is the "how to implement" part.
6. What fantastic offer (added value) can you make regarding your product—lowering prices, freebies, articles, recommendations, anything that will attract people to your business.
7. What type of guarantee do you offer? You should definitely offer a 100% Money Back Guarantee for all of your products and services.
8. What can you promise the consumer as a result of using your product?
9. What possible affiliates could you associate with?

SESSION TWENTY

Tips Booklet divisions

- After you look at your selected passion idea and the results from your mindmap, develop tips on what you know about this topic.
- Divide your tips into separate categories. (I have 12 categories as you can see from the following Index Page. You could have far fewer.)
- Add as much information as you can find to these categories. For example, if your passion is decorating, you could have categories according to seasons or rooms or themes or a combination of seasons, rooms, and themes.
- Exhaust your subject. Check every facet, then put each facet into a slot.
- Each division is a potential product.
- Your tips booklets should be able to fit into a #10 business-size envelop. They are generally printed in multiples of four, meaning four pages, eight pages, or sixteen pages. If you go beyond sixteen pages, you will have to pay extra postage to mail them. My booklets are all sixteen pages.

FOR EXAMPLE, the following is from one of my tips booklets:

(cover):
HOW TO
BE A FANTASTIC
PARENT AND
RAISE FANTASTIC
KIDS

by Gail Cassidy

(index page)

	TOPIC	PAGE
1.	Philosophy	1
2.	Attitude	2
3.	Human Relations	3
4.	Communication	4
5.	Self Esteem	5
6.	Discipline	6
8.	Parenting Treasure Tips	8
9.	Tips for Spouses	9
10.	Tips for All Family Members	10

(introductory page)

TIPS FOR PARENTS

Parenting is a wonderful and satisfying opportunity in life, but it is also one that can be filled with challenges and frustrations. From my many years teaching and raising children, I have found the following tips to be relevant for all situations, no matter what the age of the child.

Enjoy reading the tips. Highlight those you want to keep in the forefront of your mind. Enjoy every moment with your child. Your children will give you far more than you will give to them. Their unique ideas, their individual perspectives, and their humor will provide you with the gift of never-ending fond memories.

This is the most important job you will ever have. These tips will make raising your children considerably easier.

Good luck on your new, exciting adventure. What a wonderful time this is!! You have the opportunity to make the world a better place by the child you are adding to it. Have fun!!! Enjoy every precious moment!

Tomlyn Publications
Gail Cassidy

voice: 908 654-5216
gail@coachability.com
https://www.cassidycourses.com

Copyright 2020

(page one)
PHILOSOPHY

1. See the invisible tattoo on child's forehead that reads: **"PLEASE MAKE ME FEEL IMPORTANT."**
2. Find at least one happening in each day to be grateful for, and let your child know.
3. Look for positives in every child.
4. Recognize the specialness of personality and physical diversity. Every child is different from every other child, and that's special.
5. Provide an atmosphere conducive to acceptance and validation.
6. Vary your daily and weekly activities. Do something different that your children will remember.
7. Remember, humans of any age have limited attention spans. Be aware of your expectations.
8. Get children involved with family chores. Teaching responsibility must begin early.

9. The greatest gift you can give children of all ages is to let them know that they are lovable and that they are worthwhile.
10. Learn the Serenity Prayer: "God, grant me the serenity to accept the things I cannot change, courage to change the things I can and the wisdom to know the difference."
11. "See" and/or "feel" your gratitude regarding your children before the day starts via positive self talk.
12. Be (or act) enthusiastic about everything you do. It's contagious; it carries over to the children.

[END OF EXAMPLE]
A complete adapted *Success Teams* booklet can be found in Session 26.

I have 12 variations of my one basic booklet, each directed toward and adapted for a different audience: police, realtors, trainers, graduates, school boards, non-profit agencies, etc. These booklets contain information I feel strongly about.

What is it you feel strongly about? You don't have to have a polished, ready-to-print booklet, just an outline of your passion. With an outline, you can add the details as you delve deeper into your subject.

I have a very talented, artistic friend, Anthony Ferrara, for whom I made a mock-up booklet. He has the talent to make any place look beautiful. He can buy a scrape of material and turn it into something magnificent. In his mockup tips booklet, I listed topics such as *living room, dining room, Christmas holidays, Easter, summertime, patio ideas, accessories, etc.* He is working on his booklet as a promotional item to sell his decorating services.

TO RECAP, COMPLETE THE FOLLOWING:

My passion is _____

My product is _____

My booklet contains these topics: _____

You have your passion, your product, and your booklet. Now, let's look at how you can make others aware of the existence of your business.

SESSION TWENTY-ONE

(Projects to think about for the future)

WEBSITE or BLOG development for profit center

- Decide on a distinguishing name that will allow customers to know what you do.

A good example is "automotiveresearchservice.com" in comparison to any of the following: 4nra.com, 8tuv.com, a2zu.com, ayem.org, b-cx.com, b2he.com, biqu.net, biqu.org, ccil.net, cokr.org, cyah.net, dh2o.net, dh2o.org, ei41.com, gory.org, hjha.com, htus.org, ih10.net, ip65.com, ip67.com, ja-1.net, ja-1.org, ksok.net, ksok.org, o1ap.com, o1uk.com, psbb.org, qwke.com, timl.org, uonq.com, urus.org, uxxi.com.

Can you tell what any of the domains do? This list is a very small segment of the daily names I receive listing domain names that have expired.

If you have chosen a name, such as *coaching.com* that you would like, go to www.godaddy.com or www.register.com or www.networksolutions.com or any of a dozen domain registrars and type in the name. *Coaching.com* probably has been taken, but you will be given dozens of names close to your choice that might appeal to you. Keep trying until you come up with something you like. I use two domains: www.godaddy.com and www.networksolutions.com - both are reliable.

You may want to register your name as the hosted site. You can then purchase as many other names as you'd like and have them directed to your site. My main, hosted domain is http://www.coachability.com. I used to have a number of other names that go to my site, such as GailCassidy.com, DiscoverYourPassion.com, Profit-From-Your-Passion.com, RetireToYourPassion.com, TheValidatingMentor.com, OneTalkFitsAll.com, and YouCannotNOTCommunicate.com. For lack of use, I have dropped some of the names.

With one main domain, you pay only one monthly or yearly fee.

- Plan your site carefully before contacting a web designer or even if you plan to put it up yourself, but don't worry about your site being perfect. You can always make changes later.
- If you plan to teach a course or courses online, I highly recommend Kajabi.com as your software platform. You can upload your courses, send emails, blogs, promotions, hold webinars, set up a community, and lots more - all for one monthly fee. You can do it yourself with little technology expertise.
- Your site could be your brochure or it could be interactive, according to what you desire.
- Register with search engines. Google "search engines" or enter "top ten search engines" or go to www.searchenginewatch.com.

- Use good key words so search engines can locate you. You can check on the effectiveness of the words you use by checking the information available to you through google keywords.
- Words for the main index page title are very important. For example, because I do e-book publishing, I could use the following words: *mail order, mail-order, self publishing, self-publishing, self publish, self-publish, publishing, information, mail order publishing, mail-order publishing, mail order publishing, training, manuals, manual, speaking, imaging, public speaking, writing, writer, booklets, how-to books, how to books, book publishing,* etc., etc. Including commonly misspelled words is also helpful in case someone does misspell while searching.
- To get ideas for your keywords, Google the primary word representing what you are selling. When I entered the word "speaking" I found it is used **455,000,000** times (these numbers vary daily).
- For more information on developing web sites, google "Website development" and look over what's available. Right now there are **3,120,000,000** responses to "Website development."

BLOGS

Many on-line entrepreneurs are ignoring websites and using blogs to get their message out.

I googled "blogging platforms" and got the following:

Here are the popular blogging platforms found when I googled "blogging platforms."

1. WordPress.org
2. Constant Contact Website Builder
3. Gator
4. WordPress.com
5. Blogger
6. Tumblr
7. Medium
8. Squarespace
9. Wix
10. Ghost

Choosing The Best Blogging Platform – What to Look for?

Before diving in the list, it is helpful to know what you're looking for in a blogging platform.

As a beginner, you'll want a blogging platform that's easy to set up, has a low learning curve, and doesn't require any coding skills.

You'll also need to think about what kind of blog you want to create, now and in the future.

As your blog grows, you may want to change the look of your site and add more features for your growing audience. That means it's important to choose a blogging platform that's flexible, with room to grow.

Starting off with the wrong platform can make it very difficult to switch later on.

Lastly, even if you don't have plans to make money blogging right now, it's smart to make sure you have the option to do so in the future.

A worthwhile article to read on Examples of Blogs, Inspiration to help you create your own blog, go to https://makeawebsitehub.com/examples-of-blogs/ by Jamie.

SESSION TWENTY-TWO

E-zine ideas on profit centers

- Jot down ideas or keep a journal of ideas about every article and book you read, every TV program you watch that is related to your topic that can then serve as a resource for your e-zine or newsletter to your "list."
- Write about what you've read, seen, experienced and submit it to other e-zines in order to become known in your area. What you want are more hits to your website or blog that readers can easily find in the attribution you include at the end of any article you write and give away.
- Use articles as the basis for your own E-zine.
- Include personal stories of people who have used or who have benefited from your product, knowledge, service.
- Include testimonials whenever possible. The goal is to establish your credibility and trust.
- Keep your ezine relatively short. If it is too long, people will not spend the time reading it.
- Write as you speak. Don't use words others won't understand. If you prefer speaking to writing, download the app, Temi which transcribes your speaking for $.10 a minute and gets it back to you within minutes. Rev is another app which is more expensive ($1/minute) but also has more professional uses.
- Send your ezine weekly or bi-monthly. Monthly is too long—people forget; daily is too overwhelming.
- To become thoroughly proficient at developing and registering e-zines, go to Ezine Articles Submission for further clarification.
- If you don't have an e-zine, write articles with your attribution (name and how to reach you) at the end. If readers are interested in what you have to say, they will go to your site/blog.
- If you google "article services" you will be led to **4,500,000,000** site possibilities.

SESSION TWENTY-THREE

(Be aware that URL's change frequently. If a site does not work,
google the topic and you will find more options.)

Selling knowledge ideas: (Google each of the following topics as domains change frequently.)

- **Write a paragraph describing your e-zine and submit it to newsletter announcement site. Google "newsletter announcement sites."** http://emailuniverse.com takes you to a site with a variety of articles about email newsletter publishing strategies.
- **For a multiple e-zine site,** google the same,
- **Get listed on the e-zine search/directories**
- **Register to win free e-zine advertising** to over 100,000 subscribers by googling "free e-zine advertising,
- **Market services specifically geared toward increasing e-zine subscription base:** http://www.directoryofezines.com
- **Free resources for finding e-zines to subscribe to and advertise in. Google " Free resources for finding e-zines to subscribe to and advertise in."**
- **Announce your e-zine on these websites:**
  http://www.ezinehub.com
  http://www.newsletteraccess.com
  http://www.marketingforsuccess.com
  http://www.virtualpromote.com
  http://www.ezinesearch.com
  http://emailuniverse.com/bestezines
- **Google "How to buy ezine subscribers"** http://www.NewslettersForFree.com
- **To sell e-zine ad space** http://www.BestNewsletters.com
- **Columns/articles:** write one weekly and submit to other e-zines-make yourself known. Submit to your local newspaper or magazine.
- **Google "Free ezine for article submission"** to find where you can submit your articles.

SESSION TWENTY-FOUR

Spend some time googling various aspects on ezine articles:

- **Where to post newsworthy article submissions.**
- **Where to subscribe for ezine**
- **Sites that post articles, google The top ten article posting sites."**
- **E-book internet resources**
- **Publicity accessible mailing lists**
- **Opt-in lists**
- **Free ezine**

At end of each article you submit, mention that people are free to re-publish the article as long as they include your information at the end of the article. Always include the URL of your website or blog in your information box.

Gail A. Cassidy

SESSION TWENTY-FIVE

SUMMARY and WORKSHEETS

Selling services and products ideas

1. Know exactly who your audience is. This cannot be stated strongly or often enough. There is no one product or service for everyone.
2. Be clear about what makes your service/product different/better. Make sure you have benefits none of our competitors offers, e.g. a special niche, extraordinary training/background/experience. Why are you the best pest control provider?
3. Make your contacts an offer they can't refuse in the form of a coupon, free education, article, report, sample, or anything of value to a potential customer.
4. Underpromise and overdeliver. Offer a "No Questions Asked" guarantee.

- Join newsgroups related to your product/service,
- Post messages. Get yourself known.
- Go to chat rooms; post on bulletin boards.
- Register your freebies
- **List any "aha's" you have had from previous lessons.**
- **What progress have you made?**
- **Do you have any new ideas?**

Input for further development

I would love to hear from you at <u>gail@coachability.com</u> regarding any of the following topics or anything we covered in this course.

- Recommendations for next update.
- What you would like to see covered in more detail?
- What you would like to see covered in less time?
- What are your greatest challenges?
- What are your greatest fears?
- What is blocking you from starting today?

GENERAL MARKETING PRINCIPLES WORKSHEETS

(Respond to these worksheets in your Journal, and you will be well on your way to marketing on the internet.)

GENERAL PRINCIPLES RECAP

- **Know your audience**
- **Know your elevator speech**
- **Know your customers' wants and needs**
- **Have a clear message that answers their needs**
- **Know the benefits of your product or service**
- **Create a hook**
- **Have professional and personal success teams**
- **Sell <u>knowledge</u> (articles, books, workshops, seminars, talks), <u>services</u> (coaching, teaching, consulting, seminars), and <u>products</u> (software, programs, affiliate products.) to get people to buy your service or product.**

In your notebook, respond to the following:

1. **Identify your audience.**

Who?

Wants?

Motivations/Emotions?

Needs?

2. **Elevator speech (1 minute)**
3. **What is your message?**

Benefits?

Mental picture?

Impact on client?

Personal experience?

Why important?

Gail A. Cassidy

4. **What pain will be reduced, replaced?**

Ultimate advantage?

Features?

Fantastic Offer?

Guarantee?

Promise?

Brand?

Distinguishing difference?

5. **MESSAGE**

HOOK?

What's in it for me?

6. **PROFESSIONS' SUCCESS TEAM**

Personal Prospect Professional's names?

Personal names?

7. **IDEAS TO GET PEOPLE TO BUY**

Knowledge?

Services?

Products?

Web/Blog site development

PLAN:

Each section obviously will take considerable time, according to where you are in starting your business. Again, these are ideas to keep in mind for the future when you are ready to take these steps,

Step One is extremely important, in fact, an absolute necessity if you are intending an on-line business. After you decide on your product and/or service, you have to decide what you want on your web site, whether you are designing the site or a professional designer is. Take time deciding your domain name. For more ideas, type in your selected name in godaddy.com and if it is taken, you will be given a list of similar names from which you can choose.

- **Results of googling your product or service:**
- **Web site name:**
- **Web designer:**
- **Site type:**
- **Register your domain name:**
- **Credentials on your site:**
- **Testimonials:**
- **Get name and e-mail of every person who clicks through?**
- **Merchant account:**
- **Website review:**

SEARCH ENGINES

PLAN:

When you have completed your web site, this next section will take far less time. For more detailed information on this aspect of your business, google "search engines" to learn more.

- **Register with search engines.**
- **Key words:**
- **Words for the main index page title:**
- **Manually Submit to Search Engines.**
- **List your website in top search engines.**
- **E-mail signature:**
- **Pay-per-click search engine:**
- **Listed in Regional Specific Directories and Search Engines:**
- **Advertising in city guides:**
- **Track placement in search engines:**
- **Autoresponder:**

WRITING:

PLAN:

While the web site is essential, having an e-zine where you can keep in touch with your clients and where you can gather new names for your list is almost as important. Get into the habit of writing an article a week--to be used in your ezine as well as to be submitted to an articles bank where others can use it, thereby getting your attribution seen by others.

<u>E-ZINE IDEAS:</u>

- **Journal of ideas:**
- **Experiences:**
- **Articles:**
- **Personal stories**
- **Testimonials**
- **Weekly or bi-monthly:**
- **Trade ads with**
- **Paragraph describing newsletter:**
- **Submit to newsletter announcement site**
- **Get listed on the ezine search/directories**
- **Register to win free ezine advertising**
- **Free resources for finding e-zines to subscribe to and advertise in:**
- **Announce your ezine on these websites:**
- **Buy subscribers**
- **Sell e-zine ad space**
- **Columns/articles:**
- **Invited articles:**
- **Posted articles**
- **Article submissions:**

E-BOOK INFORMATION

PLAN:

If you have written a number of articles related to your business, you are in a position to create your own e-book. Look at the types of articles you've written, and arrange them in a logical sequence, e.g., "The Ten Best Ideas for Building a Boat" or "Six Ways to Get Out of a Speeding Ticket." Using a catchy title and delivering what is perceived as "of value" is another stage in your writing career. Writing as you speak will enable readers to relate to you.

- **E-book topic:**
- **Publication:**

MAILING LISTS

PLAN:

You need to get names for your ezine. The slow way is word-of-mouth and coming as a result of the attributions on articles you've written and which are found on the sites of others. You may need to look closely at the best ways to get names to your list. Check out the recommendations in the previous section and set a goal of 10,000 names. That's a great start, and that's when word-of-mouth kicks in and enables you to get additional readers who hopefully will purchase your product or service.

- **Opt-in lists**
- **Rental email lists**
- **E-mail lists where you can buy advertising:**

AFFILIATES

PLAN:

You could set up an entire business just with affiliates; however, you will probably want to add affiliates related to your business. Making your business an affiliate that others can become involved with exponentially increases your business. After you are satisfied with your web site and your articles and possibly your e-book, then you can take the next step and become affiliated. This is a great idea and not a necessity.

- **Affiliates:**
- **Affiliate Programs:**

CHATROOMS/NEWSGROUPS/BULLETIN BOARDS

PLAN:

Getting your name known/recognized in your industry gives you enhanced credibility and is more likely to attract more clients. A common term used today is "Branding." Branding is getting yourself recognized as the "go to" person in your industry. One way to meet people who matter in your field is to go to chatrooms, blogs, bulletin boards and make yourself known.

- **Related newsgroups**
- **Email Broadcast Service:**
- **Post messages.**
- **Resource for promotion:**
- **News release posting:**
- **Related Chat rooms.**
- **Bulletin Boards:**

OPT-IN MAILING LISTS

PLAN:

A great way the capture names of people who browse on your website is to have an opt-in mailing list for an e-zine or e-book you have to offer. This gives you an inexpensive way to keep in touch with your clients.

- **Send notices, updates, special offers**
- **E-mail rental lists**

<h1 style="text-align: center;">ADS</h1>

PLAN:

When you find sites related to yours and who accept advertising, it would be worthwhile to take out an ad to see if you can get readers of the related site interested in your product/service.

<h2 style="text-align: center;">FREEBIES</h2>

PLAN:

Most people love things that are free and that are relevant to their lives and/or their careers. Articles can be turned into free reports. Webinars can be recorded and made available to people on your list.

- **Freebies:**
- **Register your freebies**

<h2 style="text-align: center;">PODCASTS</h2>

Do you prefer talking to people who share your interests? Perhaps a podcast would be a fun thing to do. Google podcast directory and you will find many choices available.

Podcasts can last for a few minutes to an hour or more. You choose the topic and either talk about it yourself or invite like-minded people to join you. The variety of topics is endless. Podcasts have become so popular because they can be listened to any place or any time.

The following is an article written by Michelle Ruoff about podcast ideas:

PODCAST, GETTING STARTED
13 Creative Podcast Segment Ideas
MICHELLE RUOFF DECEMBER 27, 2018

(Permission by Live365 blog, https://live365.com/blog/13-creative-podcast-segment-ideas)

As a podcaster, you may have spent some time brainstorming segments that you can incorporate into your podcast. Even if you have a very specific podcast topic and a set format, a few segments can add some variety to your podcast and make it that much more engaging. Brainstorming segments can be challenging though, so we've compiled 13 creative segment ideas that you can use as is or personalize to add some variety to your podcast!

1. **Q & A**

Ask your listeners on social media to send in questions and randomly select a few on your podcast to answer.

2. Guest

Invite experts, friends, family, influencers, musicians, and other notable individuals to your podcast. You can have a conversation with them, have your guest give a lecture, have them takeover your podcast episode, do an interview, or have them co-host.

3. Topical News

Look up the news related to your podcast and talk about it. Even if it's not directly related, if you're interested in talking about the news, consider discussing it in a segment.

4. Recommendation

Give artist, song, album, recipe, product, tool, book, game, movie, destination, and other recommendations to your listeners. Whatever you are particularly interested in at the time, let your listeners know!

5. Fact of the Day

Do you know of or have you recently learned an interesting fact that your listeners would be interested in? Tell your listeners!

6. Story of the Day

Have an interesting story about your life, food, your house, relationships, money, animals, or anything else? Share it with your listeners!

7. Review/Recap

Review or recap a song, album, event (concert, festival, award show, sporting event, etc.), book, game, show, or movie. Anything that is relevant that you have an interest in and some knowledge about, consider reviewing it.

8. Social Media Minute

Create a hashtag and read out the posts that use that hashtag. You can engage with your listeners and have them contribute to a fun segment on your podcast.

9. Quote of the Day

Whether you have a funny or inspirational quote to share, they both make for a great segment on your podcast.

Gail A. Cassidy

10. **Spotlight**

Feature an artist, album, movie, show, destination, specific topic, or anything else that you would like to talk about more in depth. A spotlight is similar to a review, except spotlights are more based on factual information and reviews are more based on your opinions.

11. **Advice of the Day**

Have you got any advice, resources, tools, or anything else that would benefit your listeners? Share it!

12. **Requests**

Have your listeners, friends, and family submit news, topics, and other requests for you to talk about.

13. **Time Travel**

Look back at a specific podcast episode and reflect on the episode and what has changed since.

Even just one or two creative segments can make your podcast that much more engaging. Segments are a great tool to break up your lengthy or heavy content, so it is a good idea to consider adding some segments every now and then. These are just a few ideas that make as a great basis for a segment that you can personalize for your podcast. Remember, only choose segments that fit with your podcast and that you anticipate will be appealing to your audience. And, don't be afraid to expand upon these segments and make them your own, the more you personalize and own your segments, the more engaging they will be! Happy podcasting!

What would you like to share with others?

- Tennis serve information
- Golf technique
- How to build a drone
- How to master calculus
- How to bake
- How to save money
- How to build a website
- How to create an online game
- How to start a lawn business
- How to fix ——-
- How to deal with pesty siblings
- How to build ————-
- Saving our environment
- Pet care

- Gun laws
- Craft ideas
- How to declutter

There are endless ideas. What most interests you?

If you complete these worksheets, I absolutely guarantee you will
be well on your way to making money doing what you love!!!
You know your passion, and now you have a plan!

SECTION SIX

HELPFUL RESOURCES, SUCCESS TEAMS, COACHING

SESSION TWENTY-SIX

HELPFUL RESOURCES

Tips for Success as
Success Team Members

A Success Team is a small group of people dedicated not only to their own success, but also to the success of every other member in the group. Each team member is essentially a "Friendly Butt Kicker"--someone who makes sure you succeed.

Life has its ups and downs, but remember: Our perspective and our state of mind create our reality. Everything in life depends on how you look at it. To give you a silly, but apt example, "To her lover, a beautiful woman is a delight; to a monk, she's a distraction; to a mosquito, she's a good meal." When in doubt, step into another person's shoes. Here is where a Success Team can help by sharing other perspectives.

When working with Success Team Members, please remember **Tip #1, See the invisible tattoo on every human being's forehead that reads: "PLEASE MAKE ME FEEL IMPORTANT."** The best way to do this is to be encouraging and supportive.

This section will show you how!

<u>SUCCESS TEAM BASICS</u>

To maximize your chances of being successful in any endeavor, I would highly recommend you form a Success Team, a group of three to five individuals who also have goals they would like to reach. This could be done in the classroom or outside on your own time. Your goals could be as diverse as starting a business to raising a child or cleaning out the basement. What you each have in common is a desire to get something done.

The primary objective of each team member is to keep every other team member on the path he chooses to follow, and, at the same time, be successful in the pursuit of his dreams. Team members do not have to know one another; they just have to have a goal they want to achieve.

Team members allow members to progress at their own pace, but they will not let them quit in spite of the reasons that have stopped them in the past--too many things to do, sick child, an illness, tiredness, bad mood, interruptions, and so much more. The fact is life is full of interruptions.

STEP ONE: In this class, everyone is intent on reaching their goals. Once a week, divide into your groups of three or four.

STEP TWO: Divide the time available by four if four are in the group which would probably be ten minutes per person.

STEP THREE: Emphasize *perseverance*, which means "keep going" no matter what!

STEP FOUR: Divide equally the time allowed each member and stick to it. Use a timer (four members in a 50 minute class period means each person gets 10 minutes to present his dreams/goals, problems, progress and/or plans.)

STEP FIVE: A good tool to use when addressing problems stated by a Success Team member is the problem-solving formula:

- What's the problem?
- What's the cause(s) of the problem?
- What are some solutions?
- What is the best solution?

STEP SIX: The team helps each member set targets to be achieved by a specific date, chosen by the member.

STEP SEVEN: The team goes to work on the goal setter's problem in two ways: 1) helping him transform big, vague obstacles into precise ones that can be tackled strategically, and 2) helping him plan backward to the first steps that can be taken in the coming week. It is the team's job to come up with useful first steps.

STEP EIGHT: The goal setter's job is to write all the steps and schedule as many as can realistically be taken in the upcoming week. Each person works on her goals as quickly or as slowly as she chooses.

STEP NINE: The team should look for negative body language and listen for negativity, i.e., "This is stupid." Encouragement, understanding, and validation is what the member needs, along with a nudge to keep going.

STEP TEN: Effective measures used by teams include brainstorming where any idea is worth considering, skill sharing where team members offer each other the benefit of their professional or amateur skills, rehearsals, or role-playing in order to work out situations.

Teams stay together only for as long as they need to fulfill their goals. Some members may choose to belong to more than one team, each working on a different goal.

To make it easier to interact with one another and be successful dealing with each other, each member of the Success Team may want a copy of these 150 tips and quotes.

GENERAL PHILOSOPHY OF LIVING

1. See the invisible tattoo on everyone's forehead that reads: **"PLEASE MAKE ME FEEL IMPORTANT."**
2. Find at least one happening in each day to be grateful for.
3. Look for positives in every person.
4. Recognize the specialness of diversity.
5. Provide an atmosphere conducive to happiness, e.g. pictures, lighting, comfort, simplicity, etc.
6. Vary your daily activities. Do something different that will revitalize you.
7. Remember, humans of any age need breaks.
8. Know that everyone you meet has something special to offer.
9. Living in the moment is where you find happiness.
10. Learn the Serenity Prayer: "God, grant me the serenity to accept the things I cannot change, courage to change the things I can and the wisdom to know the difference."
11. "See" and/or "feel" your positive day before you climb out of bed. Use positive self talk.
12. Be (or act) enthusiastic about everything you do. It's contagious; it carries over to the people in your life.
13. Accept people as they are, and then provide the atmosphere for them be happy and grow.
14. Learn from every colleague, every friend.
15. Ask yourself, "Does it really matter?"
16. Being right does not always work, as illustrated in this brief poem:
17. *Here lies the body of William Jay, who died maintaining his right of way. He was right, dead right as he sped along, but he's just as dead as if he were wrong.*
18. **HAVE FUN!**

ATTITUDE

19. Park your ego at the door; it hinders relationships with team members and family.
20. Give your team members and family a reason to check their negative attitudes at the door also.
21. Know that people "mirror" you. They reflect what they see, hear, and feel from you.
22. Shake things up. Make changes. "If you always do what you have always done, you'll always get what you've always got."
23. Show people through your own example what fun having a great attitude is.
24. Be patient.
25. Positive attitudes are catching wherever you are.
26. Show respect to get respect.
27. Know that attitude is a choice everyone makes every day.
28. Explain that people cannot help what happens to them, but they are **always** in charge of their responses.
29. Remember, there is a pause between stimulus and response. Choose your response carefully.
30. Ask yourself why you are **choosing** to be unhappy, bored, tired, sad, happy.
31. Know that attitude is the steering mechanism of the brain. Body language can lead to attitude.
32. Practice changing your attitude by sitting or standing straight, with your head up and a smile on your face. It does work!

33. Know that it is the attitude of our hearts and minds that shape who we are, how we live, and how we treat others.

34. Help friends and family to recognize their specialness.

35. Success is feeling good about yourself every single day. That is attitude.

36. Know and share with your friends and family that true power is knowing that you can control your attitude at all times.

HUMAN RELATIONS

37. Treat everyone as if he or she were your friend's best friend.

38. Never talk down to anyone.

39. Find what is special about every person you meet.

40. **SMILE!** It warms a room.

41. Use tact when responding to a challenging person. The rewards outweigh "being right."

42. Know that it is not okay for people to feel your negativity. Your negativity is your choice.

43. Be 100% fair at all times--no exceptions.

44. Keep in mind that perception is reality--yours and your friends and family's.

45. Treat every person as you wish to be treated.

46. Understand that no one **wants** to be wrong.

47. **Everyone desperately wants to feel special.**

48. Remember that people gravitate toward things that are pleasurable and avoid things that are painful. Make Success Teams pleasurable.

49. LISTENING is the greatest compliment.

50. Try to understand before being understood.

51. Show genuine appreciation to people you work and live with.

52. Begin corrective action with sincere and honest recognition of what has been done correctly.

53. Never embarrass anyone. Allow the person to save face.

54. Use encouragement. Make the error seem easy to correct.

55. Don't be afraid to admit your mistakes. It will make you appear more human.

56. Show respect for every person's opinion.

57. Challenge people to be the best that they can be.

58. Make **SINCERITY** your No. 1 priority.

COMMUNICATION

59. Set standards in your everyday life and share them with your friends and family.

60. Know the purpose and importance of what you are doing.

61. Set high expectations.

62. Know that 55% of all messages comes from the body. Notice how you can tell your special someone is in a bad mood without any words being spoken.

63. Know that 38% of the message comes from the voice: inflection, intonation, pitch, speed, e.g., "I didn't say he stole the exam." Seven words equals seven meanings.

64. Know, you **cannot NOT** communicate.

65. Recognize that we don't all see the same thing when looking at the same thing.

66. Know also that we don't all hear the same things even when listening to the same words.
67. Control your thoughts; your feelings come from your thoughts; therefore, you can also control your feelings! Choice is control.
68. Take responsibility for what you say and how you say it.
69. Listen for the message, yet know that body language can be interpreted as only a clue to the meaning of the message, e.g., arms crossed in front of chest could mean blocking you or could mean person is actually cold or comfortable.
70. Learn to lead rather than to try and overcome resistance.
71. Communicate your enthusiasm through your body and voice.
72. "One who is too insistent on his own views, find few to agree with him." -Lao-Tze
73. Speak with a warm heart.

SELF ESTEEM

74. Know that a person with high self-esteem does not need to find fault with others.
75. Remember that people find fault with others when they feel threatened, consciously or unconsciously.
76. Know that self-esteem is not noisy conceit. It is a quiet sense of self-respect, a feeling of self-worth. Conceit is whitewash to cover low self-esteem.
77. Remember, people have two basic needs: to know they are **lovable** and **worthwhile**.
78. Remember, it is a person's feeling about being respected or not respected that affects how s/he will behave and perform.
79. Helping people build their self-concept is key to being a successful parent and/or friend.
80. Know that your words have power to affect a person's self-esteem.
81. Each person values himself to the degree s/he has been valued.
82. Words are less important in their affect on self-esteem than the judgments that accompany them.
83. The attitude of others toward a person's capacities is more important than his possession of particular traits.
84. Bragging people are asking for positive reflections.
85. Masks are worn to hide the "worthless me."
86. Low self-esteem is tied to impossible demands on the self.
87. A person's own self-acceptance frees him or her to focus on others, unencumbered by inner needs.
88. The single most important ingredient in a nurturing relationship is honesty.
89. Ask this: "If I were to treat my friends as I treat my children, how many friends would I have left?"
90. Avoid mixed messages. Be clear in your statements of expectations.

BOUNDARIES

91. Tolerate no disrespect.
92. Be consistent in enforcing rules.
93. Set boundaries.
94. Find opportunities for each other to improve the quality of his/her work.
95. Differentiate between the action and the person.
96. Uncover and address, when possible, the reasons for the person's poor performance.

97. Make sure people you work with have the skills to succeed.

98. Focus, as often as possible, on what is right rather than what is wrong.

99. Give plenty of recognition for the unique gifts of each person.

100. Keep in mind that you have power in the present moment to change your thoughts, feelings, and attitude about the past.

101. Take control of your life by focusing on the present.

102. Remove the word "try" from your vocabulary. "Try" to pick up a pencil. Either you do or you don't.

103. Find the lesson or value in unacceptable situations.

104. Know that you have choices in spite of your past experiences.

105. Turn problems into a learning opportunity.

106. Have a clear vision of where you are going.

107. Approach problematic situations with relaxed confidence.

108. Respond thoughtfully to challenging and/or problem situations.

109. Avoid making judgments.

110. Always see beyond your own point of view.

111. Encourage habits of thought conducive to growth in understanding others, to think outside the box.

LIFE'S TREASURE TIPS

112. Begin to be now what you will be hereafter. - St. Jerome

113. Know that you too are special.

114. Enjoy each day and each moment of life.

115. Correct someone by citing two positives for every negative.

116. Live in the present.

117. Be alert for moments of gratitude.

118. Show lively enthusiasm!

119. Create an atmosphere of fun.

120. Build on successes.

121. Create a routine with varied activities.

122. Visualize doing well.

123. Be relaxed.

124. Remember, "You are what you choose today." -Dyer.

125. Give yourself opportunities to succeed.

126. Provide a safe atmosphere.

127. Validate yourself frequently.

128. Your reality is what you make it to be.

129. Polish your people skills.

130. Hone your communications skills.

131. Take excellent care of yourself.

Gail A. Cassidy

MORE TIPS

132. Work towards feeling good about yourself. It is man's highest goal.

133. Always do what you feel is right or true.

134. Your actions reveal your values.

135. Your thought is the most powerful force in your universe. "Nothing is either good or bad but thinking makes it so." -Shakespeare

136. Whatever you dwell on expands.

137. Work toward goals that cause you to feel a sense of mastery.

138. Write a list of everything you have accomplished or have been recognized for in your life. Add to it whenever you think of something new. Read it when the going gets tough.

139. Have a clear sense of purpose in life.

140. Clarify your goals and focus on them.

141. Be a risk taker. Step outside your comfort zone. Try something new.

142. Positive expectations are the single, most outwardly identifiable characteristics all successful people possess.

143. You can train yourself to think more positively by training yourself to choose what you pay attention to and what you say about it, both to yourself and others.

144. Whatever you believe, picture in your mind, and think about most of the time, you eventually will bring into reality.

145. Your self-image is the most dominant factor that affects everything you attempt to do.

146. Nothing is more exciting than the realization that you can accomplish anything you really want that is consistent with your unique mix of natural talents and abilities.

147. Remember, "Change your thoughts and you change your world." -Norman Vincent Peale.

WORTHY QUOTES

148. Beliefs have the power to create and the power to destroy. -Robbins

149. The ancestor to every action is a thought. -Emerson

150. Things do not change; we change. -Thoreau

151. The greatest discovery of my generation is that human beings can alter their lives by altering their attitudes of mind. -Wm. James

One tool that may help members of a Success Team stay on track and fulfill their commitments is the following form. Each member makes copies, completes the commitments before each session in order to make the session run smoothly. Having every member complete the form before the session will greatly enhance the effective use of time.

SUCCESS TEAM PREPARATION FORM

What I have accomplished since our last session:

What I didn't get done, but intended to:

The challenges and problems I'm facing now:

Opportunities that are available to me right now:

I want to work on with Success Team:

COMMITMENTS FOR next meeting:

Additional Notes:

Gail A. Cassidy

SESSION TWENTY-SEVEN

COACHING

Coaching is a field that attracts people from all backgrounds: sports, education, sales, musicians, artists, and many many more.

Coaches are not therapists. Therapists delve into your past to attempt to remedy the present. Coaches work from the present and elicit from the client the best ways to move forward.

Coaches are not to give answers and/or suggest plans. Coaches, student or adult, want to get the answers and plans from their clients. The coach can help clients remove obstacles in their path to success. They enable clients to see what they are tolerating in life that is impeding their progress. And all of this information comes from the client.

It's always easier to find remedies for other people's problems than your own.

Clients usually are in touch with their coaches once a week for a half-hour to one-hour session. Many coaches use a questionnaire for their clients to complete each week to make sure they are on course.

Coaches listen and engage in conversations. They actually help the client reveal themselves to themselves.

If you cannot form a success team, divide the class into twos and have kids coach one another. Pairing opposites to work with one another, each being the other's coach, is an opportunity for each to take a lead role, Their goal is to see what his or her peer is not seeing.

Coaches usually have specialties. My specialty is helping people explore their passion and fine tuning their communication skills. Other specialties may be corporate coaching, small business coaching, cancer-help coaching, ADD coaching, exercise coaching, and numerous other niches.

SESSION TWENTY-EIGHT

SIMPLIFIED SUMMARY

How many times have you resolved to do something and, in spite of your best intentions, just didn't do it? You make excuses—"I'll start tomorrow, after school is over, when my grandparents leave, after the holidays, after I lose weight, when I have enough money, when I'm on vacation?" Or you say you can't start now because of your sports activities, sick aunt, mom, dad, friends, etc. We all can relate. We've all done it, but now it's time to change.

Today you have the opportunity to make a huge difference in your life, and you already know how to do it. Let's review what you have to do to make your new life happen:

1. **COMPLETE AS MUCH AS YOU CAN OF THIS MANUAL NOW!** Take responsibility for all that goes on in your life, and, if necessary, delegate tasks to others so you can get to do your work right now.

2. **CLARIFY YOUR VISION**. Have a picture in your head of your passion (goal) and how you will implement it. Be clear on what you want to do and how it will look and feel to you. Be aware of the particular values this vision validates, and be sure your goals do not violate any of your most important values--internal or external.

3. **IDENTIFY WITH YOUR PASSION.** Live as if your passion has been put into effect. Feel the excitement of the journey. The journey is where the excitement lies. Follow the words of St. Jerome, "Begin to be now what you will be hereafter."

4. **WRITE YOUR VISION/PASSION ON A CARD.** Read it every morning and every night. Attach an emotion of excitement to your reading. Eventually you won't need to look at the card. You'll be able to recite your passion from memory and have it accompanied by that great feeling of excitement that permeates your body.

5. **MAKE A LIST OF WHAT YOUR PASSION WILL COST.** What are you willing to give up? --a little television at night, a weekend or two, shopping, reading novels, sleeping late. Everything has a price. What are you willing to pay to have your dream come true?

6. **KEEP THE NEGATIVE THOUGHTS AT BAY.** Each time a negative thought pops into your head, say "Cancel-Cancel" The first cancel is for the thought; the second is for the recognition of the thought.

7. **TELL YOUR DREAMS ONLY TO THOSE WHO WILL BE SUPPORTIVE.** You don't need any nay-sayers at this point. Life has more than enough of them. A little negativity from those you care for can open the door to self-sabotaging doubt.

8. **COMMIT TO YOUR DREAM--STAY FOCUSED.** Keep the picture in your mind of how your life will look when you implement your passion. Establish a system so that every day you are reminded of where you are going. Do this by having cards posted around the house and/or office, lists of steps to take, recorded motivational information, quotes, pictures, your columns listing experience, skills, knowledge, and gifts--anything necessary to keep you on track--focused.

Gail A. Cassidy

9. **PRACTICE YOUR RELAXATION/VISUALIZATION EVERY DAY.** This daily routine is good for you physically and mentally and has the added benefit of moving you closer to your dream.

10. **KNOW THAT YOU CAN BE WHAT YOU WANT TO BE.** Know it in the depths of your heart. Remember, Your imagination is more important than knowledge, and the words of Norman Vincent Peale, "Change your thoughts and you change your world." And one last author, Wayne Dyer, wrote "You are what you choose today." Choose wisely, believe in your dream, and it will come to be.

**In Section Eight we will explore these points in depth and learn
The Six Secrets to Success.**

SECTION SEVEN

JOB SEARCH PREPARATION
INTERVIEWING

SESSION TWENTY-NINE

JOB SEARCH PREPARATION

Your passion may be one that is found in the future working for someone else, either in a small business or in a corporate setting. If so, you will no doubt have to go through the job search and interviewing process. If you do need to interview, you will need a few days to complete the following session. If you do not need to apply for a job or be interviewed, skip this section.

This section walks you through the entire job search process. Use the steps you need to take you to where you want to go. The time it will take you to complete this section depends on what it is you need to do. Work at your own pace, so that you can find the perfect place to practice your passion.

This Section covers the following:

- Planning your job search
- Finding jobs through the classified ads and networking
- Writing a cover letter
- Writing your resume
- Completing a job application
- Preparing for the interview
- Doing an actual interview

Whether you are looking for a full-time job, a part-time job, or a summer job, the areas in which you need to develop proficiency are the same. You should have a plan and an idea of how long you can be without a job. Remember, there are always temporary agencies that will place you in a job for a short time. Spend time on developing your resume and preparing for your interviews.

But remember, maintaining a positive attitude is one of the best things you can do for yourself. Your attitude shows through your nonverbal communication and, if negative, will come through in an interview. An old Dale Carnegie saying is "Act enthusiastic and you'll be enthusiastic."

FINDING THE RIGHT JOB HOW?

Most people looking for a job rely on traditional job search methods such as:

- Reading the help wanted ads in newspapers
- Going to company personnel offices and filling out applications
- Sending out resumes
- Going to local employment services offices

More than that is needed. If you are not immediately successful finding your desired job using the traditional job search methods, you could lose your motivation.

In addition to using the traditional methods of finding employment, develop a personal job search network. Networking is one of the most effective ways to find a job. Begin by defining the group of people you know.

- Friends
- Relatives
- Classmates
- Members of clubs and organizations
- Friends of friends

Tell everyone you meet what type of job you are looking for. People enjoy helping people. Let them help you.

There are six rules for successful networking:

1. **Get started**. The only criteria for someone to be in your network is that you talk to them. Set up a meeting and make sure you explain in simple terms what you are looking for.
2. **Present yourself well.** Be friendly, well organized, and polite.
3. **Learn something from each contact**. Even if you do not get a job lead from the meeting, find out all you can about the industry.
4. **Get two referrals**. This is essential in expanding a job search network.
5. **Follow up on all referrals**.
6. **Write a thank you note** to the person you talked to in your network.

You could have been a perfect student and have had outstanding recommendations, but companies receive so many applications that they frequently overlook the perfect candidate. That is why networking is so important. What could be more effective than a personal recommendation!

STEP ONE

EVALUATION: Self-evaluation is the first step in your job search plan. Answer the following questions thoroughly:

- What type of job do you most want?
- What are you best at doing?
- What do you believe you should do?
- What are you willing to do?

"TELL ME ABOUT YOURSELF." This commonly-asked question can be a brain tranquilizer, disabling you from responding effectively, especially if you are not prepared to answer such a broad

Gail A. Cassidy

question. Prepare in categories: past employment, education, qualifications, or any category you believe your perspective employer wants to hear.

ON A SEPARATE SHEET OF PAPER, WRITE one succinct paragraph about yourself--your interests, your experience, your qualifications, anything that would be of interest to a potential employer. (Check your "Skills" page from earlier in this book for ideas on what you can do and like to do.) Be able to use the essence of this paragraph at any time. This will help you keep your goal in the forefront of your mind. This could be your one-minute "elevator" speech in response to "What do you do?" If I were asked this question, I would say, "I provide validation, direction, and communication skills for my clients." I could then elaborate on "validation" by discussion my book, *The Validating Mentor*. "Direction" refers to this book, and "communication skills" refers to my book, *You Cannot NOT Communicate*.

Take some time and write your elevator speech that you can recall and recite at a moment's notice.

STEP TWO

CLASSIFIED NEWSPAPER ADS:

1. Look at the Sunday newspaper's classified ad section. Find a job that sounds like something you would like. For the purposes of this segment of the course, any ad that is close to what you want to do will suffice.
2. Cut out a couple or few ads that you can use for practice.

COVER LETTER:

The purpose of a cover letter is to initiate communication with a potential employer. The major objective of the cover letter is to obtain a personal meeting with the employer.

GENERAL RULES

1. Write to a specific person, not to a company. Call the company, ask for the name of the appropriate person, get the title and mailing address and always check spellings.
2. Always use the appropriate business letter format.
3. Recommended format:
   a. Paragraph #1: Introduce yourself. State your job objective and how you learned about the job opening.
   b. Highlight specific skills and qualifications you have to offer your potential employer.
   c. Tell why you think you are the appropriate candidate for this position. Include personal accomplishments and achievements.
   d. Ask for the opportunity to meet with the prospective employer. Include your phone number and address. Tell them you will call in a specified amount of time to set up an appointment.
4. Type your cover letter on good quality stationery with a matching envelope. The standard 8 1/2 by 11 inch paper size is used along with off-white paper that matches your resume.

GUIDELINES FOR A COVER LETTER

Sherry North
547 Elm Street
West Chester, NJ 07099
(908) 897-7645

Current Date

Mr. Thomas Larkin, President
Calendar Supply Company
2356 North Avenue
Scotch Plains, NJ 07076

Dear Mr. Larkin:

First Paragraph: State the reason for your letter, the specific position or type of work for which you are applying and tell how you learned about the job opening (newspaper, friend, employment agency).

Second Paragraph: State why you are interested in this position, the company, its products or services, and what you can do for the employer, e.g. why should he hire you? If you recently graduated from high school or college, explain how your academic or practical background makes you a qualified candidate for the position. Point out any specific achievements or unique qualifications you have. You can include personal characteristics such as people skills, writing skills, and communication skills. Try not to repeat the same information that is found in your resume.

Third Paragraph: Refer the reader to your enclosed resume that details your qualifications, training, and experience.

Fourth Paragraph: Indicate your desire for a personal interview and your availability. Repeat your telephone number and encourage a response. You may also state that you will call him in a few days to set up a date.

Sincerely,

Enclosure

Gail A. Cassidy

SAMPLE COVER LETTER

Sherry North
547 Elm Street
West Chester, NJ 07099
(908) 897-7645

Current Date

Mr. Thomas Larkin, President
Calendar Supply Company
2356 North Avenue
Scotch Plains, NJ 07076

Dear Mr. Larkin:

In the January 26 issue of the <u>Star Ledger</u>, I saw an opening advertised in your marketing department. I would like to apply for the position as marketing photographer. I believe my training and experience would be beneficial to your company.

As someone who appreciates your products and as a life-long user of your company's products, I am particularly interested in being a part of your organization. I have always closely followed your advertising campaigns and have utilized some of your general techniques in the development of my own ad campaigns. My recent completion of advanced marketing art techniques at Rutgers University is timely. My new learning could, undoubtedly, be of value to your company.

In my enclosed resume, you will see the positions I have held with highly regarded organizations, where I developed successful marketing art campaigns. You will also notice that I have continued my education and am always on the lookout for new and innovative courses related to this field.

I would very much like to meet with you in the near future. I will be in town next week and will be available for an interview. I will call you Monday to see if we can set up a mutually beneficial time.

Sincerely,

Enclosure

RESUMES

Many employers are deluged with poorly constructed resumes. Employers are busy people and generally will not consider resumes that are sloppily typed, hand-written, too long, hard to read, or filled with careless errors.

Your cover letter and resume are a reflection of you, so they must be perfect. Keep in mind, the resume does not get you a job, but it may get you an **interview**. Your resume must project the message that you could be a valuable employee and that it will be to the employer's advantage to see you.

RECOMMENDATIONS FOR A GOOD RESUME
Why should I hire you?

- Clarify your job objective, related skills and experiences.
- Make every word count. If a word does not support your objective, delete it.
- Use your resume as a tool to communicate your skills.
- Use action words to create a positive impression (e.g., *organized, managed, directed, implemented*).
- Eliminate extraneous information, e.g., hobbies, weight, salary requirements.
- Keep it to one page.
- Highlight your most important accomplishments and show results you produced.
- Proofread, proofread, proofread!!! Have two or three other people proofread it.
- Use high-quality paper, 20-pound paper stock.
- Do not list references. (If you are applying to a dozen companies, you don't want to overburden the people you asked to be a reference.)
- Do not leave gaps between employment dates.

<u>RESUME PARTS</u>

All resumes should contain certain vital information including the following:

HEADING: Name address, telephone and fax numbers, e-mail address.

OBJECTIVE: Identify the market you are targeting. (Avoid using specific job titles.) Include information on skills, areas of expertise, distinctions, and the benefits you would bring to the future employer.

SKILLS: A brief summary of your most important skills, experience, and/or marketable qualities. List in order of importance.

EMPLOYMENT HISTORY: Company name, years employed, positions, responsibilities, special assignments, job description. Include information regarding your achievements and contributions to the company.

PERSONAL QUALITIES: List your transferable, adaptive, and job skills from your past jobs, e.g., "requires little supervision," "excellent interpersonal skills," "detail oriented," "learns quickly."

EDUCATION: Summary of your educational background including highest degree, area of major, university, and location.

ACTION WORDS FOR RESUME

achieved	analyzed
administered	advised
analyzed	appraised
arranged	assisted
controlled	created
balanced	built
carried	coordinated
compiled	composed
counseled	developed
delivered	demonstrated
designed	directed
established	ensured
evaluated	experimented
finalized	fostered
generated	guided
handled	helped
identified	implemented
increased	influenced
instituted	integrated
introduced	investigated
launched	located
managed	modified
negotiated	obtained
organized	operated
persuaded	planned
programmed	published
reduced	represented
restructured	revamped
revised	simplified
solved	started
supervised	trained
transferred	treated
undertook	unified
upgraded	verified
withstood	worked

Gail A. Cassidy

RESUME WORKSHEET

NAME
STREET ADDRESS
CITY/TOWN, STATE, ZIP CODE
PHONE, FAX NUMBER
E-MAIL ADDRESS

OBJECTIVE (type of position or job)

_____

_____

_____

SKILLS (teaching, writing, typing, computing, accounting)

_____

_____

_____

EXPERIENCE (include full-time, part-time, summer, volunteer, military)

_____

_____

_____

PERSONAL QUALITIES

_____

_____

_____

EDUCATION (include institution, location, degree, year of graduation)

_____

_____

Sherry North
547 Elm Street
West Chester, NJ 07099
(908) 897-7645
sherry@reliability.com

OBJECTIVE: To obtain an administrative assistant position with a firm providing challenge and opportunity for professional growth.

SKILLS: Keyboarding (80 wpm), Gregg shorthand (95 wpm), Lotus 1-2-3, iMac, Windows, Quark Express, office procedures, business communications, strong math skills

EXPERIENCE: Town Book Store, Anywhere, NJ

- Cashier, book stacker
- Responsible for handling money and checking out nightly
- Maintained inventory
- Ordered new books
- Designed special displays for window

PERSONAL QUALITIES:

Organized, reliable, self-starter, excellent interpersonal skills, learns quickly, meets deadlines, responsible

EDUCATION: Anywhere High School, Anywhere, NJ
Secretarial Program, Diploma 2000
Grade Point Average 3.5, Honor's List
Outstanding Student Award
Perfect Attendance Record

Gail A. Cassidy

REFERENCES

References will be provided upon request. The following is an example.

Sherry North
547 Elm Street
West Chester, NJ 07099
(908) 897-7645
Sherry@comcast.net

REFERENCES

PROFESSIONAL
Mary Smith, Manager
Town Book Store
Anywhere, NJ 07888
(908) 454-2222

Dr. Phil McGraw, Principal
Anywhere High School
4 Norman Drive
Anywhere, NJ 07999
(908) 454-2333

Miss Sally Jones, Director
Recreation Commission
35 Morris Avenue
Anywhere, NJ 90999
(898) 394-9999

PERSONAL
Gwen Owens, Professor
Anywhere University
56 Elm Street
Anywhere, NJ 08099
(897) 345-2211

Walter Agar, Dean
Citone School
34 Harding Drive
Anywhere, NJ 0890
(877) 654-9898

JOB APPLICATION

The day has arrived. You have an appointment with a prospective employer, you have your perfectly typed resume in your folder, you are dressed appropriately for the profession you are seeking, and now you have to fill out the Application Form.

TIPS

- Bring at least two black pens (black ink makes better copies than blue ink).
- Print neatly! If your application cannot be read because of illegibility, it will not be read.
- Answer every question on the application. This shows the interviewer that you have read the application thoroughly. If a question does not apply to you, such as military service, write N/A (not applicable).
- If salary requirements are asked for, write "Open." This will better ensure that you will be seen by the interviewer. If you were to request too low a salary, you could be seen as not worthy; too high, too expensive. Play it safe.
- Remember your social security number or write it down
- For requested dates, it will be easier if you bring a copy of your resume with you.
- Be prepared to give three references, if requested. Know their names, addresses, business phone numbers, companies, titles. Also, be sure you ask permission from each reference before you use their names.

SAMPLE APPLICATION FOR EMPLOYMENT

PERSONAL INFORMATION   DATE _____

<u>NAME</u>
_____ LAST _____ FIRST _____ MIDDLE _____

<u>PRESENT ADDRESS</u>
_____ STREET _____ CITY _____ STATE _____ ZIP _____

<u>PERMANENT ADDRESS</u>
_____ STREET _____ CITY _____ STATE _____ ZIP _____

PHONE NO _____ SOCIAL SECURITY NUMBER _____

<u>REFERRED BY</u>
_____

EMPLOYMENT DESIRED

            DATE AVAILABLE   SALARY

POSITION _____ FOR WORK _____ REQUIREMENTS

_____ IF SO MAY WE INQUIRE
ARE YOU EMPLOYED NOW? _____ OF YOUR PRESENT EMPLOYER?
EVER APPLIED TO OR WORKED FOR THIS COMPANY
OR ANY OF ITS AFFILIATES BEFORE?
_____ YES _____ NO _____ WHERE _____ WHEN
                _____ YEARS _____ MAJOR OR _____

EDUCATION
NAME AND LOCATION OF SCHOOL   ATTENDED   GRADUATED   COURSES STUDIED
_____

GRAMMAR SCHOOL _____
_____

HIGH SCHOOL _____
_____

COLLEGE _____
_____

TRADE, BUSINESS OR CORRESPONDENCE SCHOOL _____
SUBJECTS OR SPECIAL STUDY OR RESEARCH WORK _____
U.S MILITARY SERVICE _____ YES _____ NO _____ PRESENT MEMBERSHIP IN NATIONAL GUARDS
ACTIVITIES OTHER THAN RELIGIOUS
(CIVIC, ATHLETIC, FRATERNAL, ETC.) _____
EXCLUDE ORGANIZATIONS THE NAME OR CHARACTER OF WHICH INDICATES RACE, COLOR, NATIONAL ORIGIN

INTERVIEWING

How you communicate determines the outcome of an interview. While your resume is important in order for the interviewer to know your background, experience, and skills, it is the interview that will determine if you are hired. You will be judged by how you communicate verbally and non-verbally. The interviewer will look for congruence; in other words, do your words match your gestures and facial expressions? He or she will also look for attitude, that indefinable feeling a person gets about you as a result of your verbal and non-verbal communication. Researchers say that a person is hired based 15% on skills and 85% on attitude.

RECOMMENDATIONS:

LEARN ABOUT THE COMPANY: Nothing is less impressive to an interviewer than having someone come in for a job who does not know what the company makes, sells, or does. Gather information about the company before the interview, either on-line or from their annual report, so you can be knowledgeable about the company's products or services, its size, locations, years of existence, reputation, philosophy, culture, as well as the names of its decision makers. Is the organization local, national, international? Are promotion opportunities available?

Failure to do your homework before the interview can make you appear less than conscientious or even uninterested.

DRESS APPROPRIATELY: Dress codes have changed in recent years, but sloppiness is never condoned or tolerated. If you are applying to a major corporation, dress for success--suit, tie, pressed and neat, shined shoes. If, however, you are applying for a job in the music industry or some other casual industry, a less formal style is certainly appropriate.

Remember, first impressions are frequently lasting impressions.

ARRIVE EARLY: If there is a traffic tie-up, you could lose a job opportunity. Plan to arrive early so you can find your way to the interviewer's office. If you have extra time, you may also find additional company materials such as reports, magazines, and advertisements about the company in the waiting room.

REMEMBER NAMES: Everyone likes to have his or her name remembered. What a wonderful compliment! Remember the names of receptionists, secretaries, and assistants for follow-up purposes. And certainly remember the name and title of your interviewer. Try to learn this information prior to the interview or during the first few moments of the session.

FIRST IMPRESSIONS: Many interviewers make their decisions about the applicant during the course of the interview, therefore, make sure you make a good first impression. Concentrate on the following:

- a firm handshake

Gail A. Cassidy

- a pleasant smile
- good grooming
- good posture (shows confidence)
- look interviewer in eye; maintain comfortable eye contact throughout
- say something first (perceived as a "take charge" attitude)
- speak with warm but professional tone
- vary the pitch and volume of your voice; avoid a monotone

BE YOURSELF: Allow your own personality to shine through. You are special exactly as you are, so don't attempt to impress the interviewer by acting differently than you regularly act.

- Avoid apologizing for things you have no control over such as your age, education, or work history.
- Never lie or exaggerate. Admit it if there is something you don't know.
- Avoid expressions such as "like"--"like you know what I mean?" or "you know" or too many "er's" and "uh's."

BE POSITIVE: Emphasize your strong points and remember, the interviewer is looking for a positive, enthusiastic person. Attitude does count. A negative person in the workplace is like a sore that never heals. Be positive. Employers can teach employees skills; they cannot teach attitude. That is the choice of each individual. Remember, attitude is 85% of the basis of your hire; skills are 15%.

Focus on what you can do for the employer.

COME PREPARED: Have questions ready about the job you are seeking. Uncover as much information as possible about the position and match your responses to support the employer's needs.

Bring with you your research information on the company, any previous correspondence, several copies of your resume, and a list of references in case you are asked for them.

MIRROR YOUR INTERVIEWER: If your interviewer is leaning forward, do the same. If he is sitting back in the chair, do the same. People are complimented by people whom they perceive as similar to them.

PRACTICE EFFECTIVE LISTENING SKILLS: Problems occur in interviews when either the interviewer or the interviewee fails to listen closely to what the other is saying. Listen closely to detect the exact nature of the interview questions, and listen to the interviewer's responses to your answers in order to gauge how well you are doing, to learn more about what is important to the interviewer, and to be able to keep conversely intelligently.

INTERESTING RESEARCH: Interviewees who failed to get hired participated in shorter interviews than did successful applicants. The successful interviewees also spoke a greater percentage of the time than did their unsuccessful counterparts. Successful applicants spoke for about 55% of the total interview time and unsuccessful ones accounted for only 37% of the words spoken during the interviews.

Seeming to control the interview also leaves an impression. Successful applicants initiated 56 percent of the comments made during the interviews, while unsuccessful applicants were viewed as followers and initiated only 37% of the comments made. It is important for the interviewee to send messages that announce that he or she is an active, not passive, respondent. (*Interviewing, Building Confidence in Communication*, Daniel Dunn Scott, Foresman & Co., Glenview, Ill).

Interviewing is salesmanship. The people who get job offers are the people who do the talking.

CLOSE: Toward the end of the interview, the main points covered are reviewed and summarized. When the interviewer is about to stand, you do also. When an interview ends well, your chances of being hired are greatly enhanced.

Thank the interviewer for the meeting, and repeat how much you are interested in the job and how well qualified you think you are for it.

FOLLOW UP: After the interview, send a brief, typed letter of appreciation for the interviewing opportunity. The letter is a good time to clarify your responses to any questions you may have handled better and to repeat your strengths and how they would benefit the company.

INAPPROPRIATE QUESTIONS

Not all interviewers are trained in interviewing skills, techniques, legalities, and etiquette. Even if a question is illegal or sensitive, it does require a response of some sort. How you respond will say a lot about you as a person.

Questions that could be discriminatory include the following:

- Birthplace
- Nationality
- Age
- Birth date
- Race
- Religion
- Marital status
- Plans for having children
- Ages of children and child care plans
- Height and weight
- History of drug or alcohol addiction
- Hobbies and outside interests
- Feelings about unions
- Disabilities or physical limitations

The Equal Employment Opportunity Commission and American Disabilities Act are intended to protect individuals under the law.

Questions that are inappropriate but not illegal to ask are as follows:

- How long have you lived at your current address?
- Do you rent or own your home?
- Who lives with you?
- Have you ever been arrested?
- Questions about your military discharge.

An interviewer could ask why you left a previous employer or what kind of reference you received or why you didn't like your previous job or how well you got along with co-workers or supervisors. **Don't complain about previous bosses or co-workers**. If you do, the interviewer will see red flags. She may conclude that you will complain about the people here also. She is looking at how you respond.

INTERVIEW QUESTIONS

Be prepared to answer questions that have no one answer. Be prepared to speak about the following:

- Tell me about yourself. (Very difficult if you are not prepared Be prepared to discuss different areas: education, experience, career desires, why you want to work here, etc.)
- How did you become interested in this career?
- Why did you choose our company?
- What is your greatest strength? Weakness? ("I work too hard" doesn't work.)
- What are your short-range goals? Long-range?
- What do you see yourself doing in five years?
- What accomplishments are you particularly proud of?
- If I were to contact one of your previous employers, what would they say about you?
- What motivates you to put forth your greatest efforts?
- How would you describe yourself?
- What do you see as the greatest challenge you would face in this job?
- How do you handle (constructive) criticism?
- What would your ideal career be?
- Why are you leaving your current position?
- What is your salary range?
- How do you feel about working overtime?
- Why should I hire you?

QUESTIONS YOU CAN ASK

- Why is this position open?
- What are the opportunities for professional growth?
- What are the opportunities for promotion?
- How would you describe your corporate environment?
- What are the responsibilities of this position?
- What resources are available for accomplishing these responsibilities?
- What is the level of authority in this position?
- How is performance measured?
- What is the company's policy regarding promoting from within?
- What is the overall structure of the department where the position is located?
- Why should I want to work for your organization?
- What type of medical and dental benefits are available?
- What is the salary offered for this position?
- When can I expect to hear from you?

Once the job offer is made, you may then want to ask additional questions:

According to the type of position, you may want to discuss additional perks, such as car availability, mileage, expense accounts, company product discount program, cafeteria or dining room privileges, professional or trade association membership dues, paid holidays, vacation time, educational assistance programs, credit unions, and anything else you would like to know.

FOLLOW-UP

The minute the interview is over, sometimes even during the interview, you should start thinking about follow-up. What can you do to further convince the interviewer that you are right for the job? The answer is the all-too-often forgotten follow-up letter, or, in some cases, phone call.

FOLLOW-UP LETTER

While thanking the interviewer is technically the reason for a follow-up letter, what you actually are doing is taking the opportunity to sell yourself further. This letter is often your last chance to convince a prospective employer that you are the right person for the job.

The sooner you write the follow-up letter and send it, the better. Don't put it off until next week. That's too late. To make the best impression, write and send it the same day as your interview or send it the following day, but date it the same day as your interview.

Since this is basically a brief thank you letter, keep it short: one page or less. In one page, remind the interviewer of the following:

- The interview itself. "Thank you for your time today. I enjoyed meeting you and discussing the graphic design position."
- Sell yourself one more time (refer directly to the specific points you discussed and examples of your qualifications) and
- Summarize or recap (essentially the same as the opening) and state that you look forward to hearing from her.

These are the three essential sections of a strong, well-organized follow-up letter.

SAMPLE FOLLOW-UP LETTER

Sherry North
547 Elm Street
West Chester, NJ 07099
(908) 897-7645
sherry@comcast.net

Current date

Mr. James Burke, Personnel Manager
Tulip Industries
34 Ames Avenue
Boston, MA 07000

Dear Mr. Burke:

Thank you for the informative interview we had today. I thoroughly enjoyed talking to you and learning more about the graphic design position at your company. The job appears to be challenging and very rewarding, exactly the type of position I am interested in.

I feel certain that my knowledge and experience with Quark Express and Photoshop would be of great benefit to Tulip Industries. If you log onto my web site, you will see even more examples than I had in my portfolio of the work that I have done using these programs. I feel confident that my qualifications would be of great value to your organization.

If I can answer any further questions, please let me know I look forward to hearing from you about your decision.

Sincerely,

Sherry North

CONCLUSION

I am a great believer in doing the best you can; there's nothing else you can do. If you believe you have prepared thoroughly for your interview and have given it your best but didn't get the job, move on to your next opportunity, and take the time to do a little self-evaluation.

CHECK OFF LIST

DID YOU

- Learn about the company beforehand?   _____
- Did you dress appropriately?   _____
- Did you arrive early?   _____
- Did you remember people's names   _____
- Was your handshake firm?   _____
- Was your smile pleasant?   _____
- Did you appear confident?   _____
- Did you initiate the conversation?   _____
- Did you maintain good eye contact?   _____
- Were you enthusiastic?   _____
- Were you positive?   _____
- Were you prepared with questions and answers?   _____
- Did you demonstrate good listening skills?   _____
- Did you send a follow-up letter?   _____

BE THE BEST THAT YOU CAN BE; AND THAT'S PERFECT!

SECTION EIGHT

SIX STEPS TO SUCCESS

(Train Your Brain)

SESSION THIRTY

SIX STEPS TO SUCCESS
The Pathway to Your Dreams
Here is the SECRET!

STEPS

1. **Discover your passion**
2. **Control your thoughts**
3. **Attach feelings/emotions**
4. **Believe**
5. **Take action with enthusiasm**
6. **Program your mind**

At this point in the course, you probably already have a good idea what your passion is. This section explains how to make your passion happen. You also are already familiar with the four **Internal Control Tools (Intuition, Thought, Attitude, and Relaxation/Visualization)** and the three **External Tools (Journaling, Self Coaching, and Mindmapping).** You are familiar with Profit Centers, Marketing Basics, and even Success Teams and Coaching. In other words, you know what to do and how to do it. **Sometimes, however, "knowing" is not enough.**

Perhaps you want to stop smoking but continue to smoke. You may want to be thin and continue eating unhealthful foods. Your passion may be leading seminars on playing the guitar, but you haven't developed the program. Perhaps you have the program but have not done anything with it. Why? Why is there a gap between what you want to do and what you do?

If you are unable to answer "Why," study this section carefully. Start with your list from your response to Question 15 that contains four parts: *My Passion, What I Want to Have, What I Want to Do, What I Want to Be.* Your identified passion is your guide. This passion is a combination of your "have," "do," and "be" list.

To bring your passion to fruition, learn how to utilize your most powerful tool - your mind. You get in life exactly what your mind focuses on, whether or not you are conscious of that fact. Just because you are good at something or have been trained to do something as your life's work, does not mean you must do it for the REST OF YOUR LIFE!

That means you can create yourself and your life exactly as you so desire.

Finding and creating your life's work, even if it is entirely different from what you have done most of your life, will bring you greater happiness and satisfaction than any other single action you can take.

Activities that you love invariably involve using skills and talents that come naturally to you. When you use your natural skills and talents, you are automatically in tune with some higher purpose. Doing what you love to do is good for you and is good for the world.

BUT FIRST, HOW CAN YOU CONSCIOUSLY CREATE THE LIFE YOU WANT?

An understanding of how the conscious and subconscious parts of your mind work is essential to implementing the **Six Steps to Success.**

You are already quite familiar with your conscious mind. It's the awareness or thinking, reasoning, logical part of your mind. You use it every waking hour to plan your day and make decisions. What you may not be aware of is that the conscious mind is also the doorway, or the opening, to the subconscious.

The subconscious mind does not think independently, but it does house your intuition, emotion, imagination, and creativity, and, of course, memory. It contains every thought, word, feeling, emotion, fear, and event in your life. It is from the subconscious that an idea pops into your mind, that a memory resurfaces, that an emotion is triggered because of a location or smell or sight.

Speakers and writers are often amazed at the power of the subconscious to furnish them with a steady flow of thoughts and ideas from books they have read in the past, even if they do not consciously remember the book or the information contained in the book.

The subconscious mind also houses your self-image, your self-concept and your personality. It never sleeps, it is a "yes" man, it is robotic, it carries out a vision, and it has no judgment. It reacts only to what it is fed through the conscious part of the mind.

The subconscious does not know right from wrong, good from bad. It accepts whatever the mind gives it. The subconscious never resists orders from the conscious mind. It carries out orders without feeling or emotion. For example, as a child, if someone you regard as an authority had repeatedly told you "you are bad or stupid," you will, in all probability, believe the description to be true and act accordingly, until you learn to believe otherwise.

In addition to housing all that has been mentioned, the subconscious has two other primary functions: 1) It maintains and preserves the well-being of your body, and 2) in times of emergency it springs into immediate action by automatically regulating your heartbeat, pumping appropriate hormones and preparing you to respond to the emergency.

So powerful is the subconscious that a person suffering from multiple personalities can be diabetic in one personality and normal in another, could have high blood pressure in one personality and have normal pressure in another.

The subconscious responds to mental pictures--real or imagined. For example, a person severely allergic to roses can wheeze and sneeze at the sight of realistic looking silk roses. That's the subconscious mind trying to protect the allergic individual. It cannot tell the difference between real and imagined events.

The subconscious mind needs goals to strive for; and once aware of the goals, will come up with creative "how to's" for the vision, dream, or goal in the conscious mind. The subconscious mind fulfills what the conscious mind seeks and always confirms what the conscious mind accepts.

In brief, the subconscious embodies the feelings, learnings, and wisdom of the past, the awareness and knowledge of the present, and the thought and vision of the future.

The subconscious supports your capabilities. You must have patience and absolute faith. In conveying your needs and desires to the subconscious, they must be presented as if the work has *already been done*. It is important for you to actually see yourself as already successful according to your conscious dream.

When you present a problem to your subconscious, you must believe the solution will be revealed to you and the correct course of action indicated; and when it is presented, you must act immediately.

You must also understand that getting to the subconscious is not easy. Envision guards protecting the entrance to the subconscious mind. You can't get there unless you lull the guards, and fortunately, there are easy ways to do that. The most common and most effective methods are relaxation, visualization, repetition, affirmations, prayer, deep breathing, and hypnosis or a combination thereof.

Your goal is to make at least one of these practices a part of your everyday life. You must remember, the subconscious mind hears everything the conscious mind hears and accepts what is heard as truth. To undo negativity or bad past programming, you can use any of the entrance methods to reprogram your subconscious, which will be covered in more detail at the end of this section.

NOW, FOR THE SIX-STEP PROCESS TO REALIZE YOUR DREAMS.

1. **DISCOVER YOUR PASSION**

The FIRST STEP in creating the life you desire is to become aware of and move toward that which you dream about, think about or visualize in your mind, that which comes naturally to you.

You must be very precise about what you want. Your imagination is your direct link to your innermost desires. Imagination gives you the ability to step outside of your self-imposed, learned limitations and create new and unlimited possibilities.

When you think about what you want to accomplish in life, you need to try to see the accomplishment or dream as reality. You have to see it before you can realize it.

If the picture in your mind is not clear, perhaps you are entertaining doubts, fears, or negative thoughts. Your imagination belongs to you, and you can imagine anything you desire.

Don't share your thoughts and dreams with others because you may be negatively impacted by the less-than-favorable reactions of others, especially those whose opinions you value. The negativity of others can dampen or destroy your efforts. When you talk about what you are going to do, you scatter the forces, thereby weakening them.

Visualization and emotion are the chief factors in influencing the subconscious mind. Clear visualization and intense concentration enables the subconscious mind to provide you with your desire. You must clearly see your goal, your dream, in your mind's eye in order to activate the subconscious to work for the fulfillment of that goal.

While you are visualizing, answer to yourself the following questions: "Where are you? Who is there with you? What is the occasion? How are you feeling, looking? What are you doing?" Picture people congratulating you and compensating you for your achievement. Feel the pride of having realized your dream. What a wonderful feeling! The combination of seeing, focusing, and feeling is what most impacts the mind. Your job is to clearly draw the picture in your mind and attach the wonderful feelings that go along with achieving your dream.

Daydreaming alone does not have the power to activate the subconscious. However, if you clearly define your daydream and add belief, emotion, imagined action, and focus to the picture, you can realize your dream, or in effect, change your daydream into a real dream, one that can be realized.

That total focus on the dream is comparable to the sun's rays shining through a magnifying glass onto combustible material such as wood or hay. If the sun's rays stay focused, eventually a fire will ignite. You want to ignite the fire of your subconscious and make your dream come true.

2. BECOME AWARE OF YOUR THOUGHTS

You must be aware of your THOUGHTS--more easily said than done. The sharper, the more urgent your desire to fulfill your dream, the sooner it will come true. The desire, however, comes in the form of thoughts. Know that you cannot have two thoughts at the exact same time. You can't keep your mind filled with negative thoughts or doubts if you have it filled with positive, powerful and creative thoughts. You have to choose which thoughts you will have. Remember, the subconscious accepts whatever you give it. You make the choice--thoughts are yours, and you can control them.

Positive thoughts generate positive, strong vibrations and visa versa. What you sow, so shall you reap. Positive thoughts generate strength. This strength is easily demonstrated by having a person think good thoughts while holding his arm straight out to the side and at the same time having someone try to push his arm down. For further evidence, have the same person stand the same way--arm outstretched and this time think negative thoughts. His arm can then be lowered using one finger.

Gail A. Cassidy

Always be aware of your thoughts and immediately cancel any that are negative. Say to yourself, "Cancel-Cancel" whenever a negative thought pops into your mind. The first "Cancel" is for the thought; the second is for the recognition or acknowledgment of the thought. "Cancel-Cancel" will make you very much aware when negativity comes into your mind.

Thoughts determine your posture, your facial expressions, your conversation, because what you are outwardly comes as a result of what you think habitually. Emerson wrote, "Every man carries in his eye the exact indication of his rank." Your mirror shows you the person others see when they look at you, and you can fashion yourself into any kind of person you would like them to see. If you believe you can, you will. If you act the part, you will become the part.

As Shakespeare said, "Assume a virtue if you have it not." In assuming a virtue, you are assuming it via your imagination. To become the person you would like to be, you need to create a mental picture of your newly conceived self, and if you continue to hold it, the day will come when you are in reality that person. And the same applies to the accomplishment of your desires. See the accomplishment or dream clearly in your mind, and it will come into being.

As individuals think and believe, so they are. Every person creates himself or herself as a result of the image of his/her own thinking and believing. As King Solomon put it, "For as he thinketh in his heart, so is he."

3. BECOME AWARE OF YOUR FEELINGS

Thoughts create reality according to the intensity of emotions involved. Emotions create energy, positive or negative, according to your thoughts. The second part of thoughts is feelings, which means emotions, energy. Feelings are emotions that are the result of thought. You must first have the thought before you can have the feeling. For example, if you won the lottery but weren't told that you had won, you couldn't be excited because you didn't know--or have the thought--that you had won. No thought, no emotion.

You create your life by feelings, not by thought. Whatever you are feeling is what you are attracting. Energy attracts like-energy, i.e., positive thoughts attract positive energy and visa versa. You get in life what you emotionally focus on--remember the magnifying glass and the sun. That is why it is so important to focus on what you want with passion and excitement. Emotion gives life to the picture.

It is the emotion attached to the picture that makes the thoughts or passion so real. The emotions begin to react to the passion as if that dream were full-blown reality. The subconscious mind does not know the difference.

You have the clear picture as revealed by your thoughts and the heartfelt emotions attached to the picture, therefore, it must be real.

By the way, you do realize that negative feelings come from guilt, fear, blame, worry, and doubt--all useless emotions, emotions you can avoid by concentrating on changing your thoughts. Remember to say, "Cancel-Cancel" to any negativity that pops into your mind.

When you feel good, you cannot experience negative emotions such as insecurity, shame, unworthiness, or inferiority. It is up to you to feel good about what you most desire in life. You must feel as if you have accomplished each desire. Taste it, feel it, smell it, and feel the elation even before your dream comes to fruition. Focus only on things that make you feel good.

Once you change your focus, you can think about what you desire and enjoy (or manufacture) the accompanying emotions.

Manifest positive feelings by getting into the feelings of wonder, appreciation, gratitude, excitement, reverence, awe, and happiness. Practice being able to bring up those feelings as you desire, especially in relationship to your dream. You can jump-start the desired positive feeling by smiling and visualizing the feeling.

4. KNOW THE IMPORTANCE OF BELIEF

Believing is the magic ingredient that leads to making your dreams come true. Nothing will happen unless you believe it will happen. The stronger your convictions and emotions, the more rapidly you will achieve your aims. As Oprah said, "The most important truth is that you become what you believe."

Dr. Emile Coue declared that imagination is a much stronger force than will power. When the two are in conflict, he said, the imagination always wins. Think of willpower as trying to swim against the tide or imagination. Eventually you will tire and end up going with the flow. Instead of will power, use your imagination, see and feel your dream, and most importantly, "know" your dream will come true.

Wishful thinking in itself is without effect, simply because the belief factor is missing. Whatever you fix your thoughts upon or steadily focus your imagination upon is what you attract.

The most sustained and continuing results come as a result of belief--when you believe it "heart and soul." It is the **belief** that brings outstanding results, sets the law of attraction into operation, and enables the dream to come true. This **belief** draws the subconscious forces into play, changing how you walk, talk, and act. As Napoleon Hill said, "Whatever the mind can conceive and **believe**, it can achieve."

5. KNOW THE IMPORTANCE OF ACTION, accompanied by ENTHUSIASM

Enthusiasm is the most powerful motivating force for change. Thomas Edison said, "When a man dies, if he has passed enthusiasm along to his children, he has left them an estate of incalculable value." How can you be enthusiastic? Dale Carnegie said, "Act enthusiastic and you'll be enthusiastic." It's that simple.

Gail A. Cassidy

You must take action if you find yourself in a less than positive state. To evoke or bring forth positive feelings, pull your shoulders back, hold your head high, smile, and then evoke from inside yourself the positive feeling you desire. It is amazing the transformation that takes place.

Stand in front of a mirror, fully erect, breathe deeply 3 to 4 times until you can feel a sense of power, strength, and determination. Look into the depths of your eyes, and tell yourself that you are going to get what you desire. State your dream aloud as if it already is in existence, so you can see your lips move and can hear your words uttered.

Make this a regular ritual and practice doing it at least twice a day. Put sayings on your desk or in your wallet, any place where you will see them during the day. As you stand in front of the mirror, keep telling yourself that you are an outstanding success and that nothing in this world can stop you. Every idea presented to the subconscious mind is going to be produced in its exact counterpart in real life, and the quicker your subconscious gets the idea, the sooner your wish becomes a picture of what you desire.

Physically, emotionally, and psychologically, you create through activity and movement whatever you hold as clear and compelling in your mind. As long as you hold that picture, you are drawn to it. Amazingly, you become aware of the steps you need to take in order to progress toward your goal. Picture each step clearly, see yourself taking that step, and then executing it perfectly. Do this every single day. Remember the magic word--**FOCUS**!

If you have definitely decided what you want and have a definite goal for yourself, consider yourself fortunate, for you have taken the first step that will lead to success. As long as you hold on to the mental picture of your dream and begin to develop it with action, nothing can stop you from succeeding, for the subconscious mind never fails to obey any order given to it clearly and emphatically.

The fact is, you move toward what you think about. Again, believe Napoleon Hill's famous line, "Whatever the mind can conceive and **believe**, it can achieve."

6. LEARN HOW TO BYPASS THE CONSCIOUS MIND.

You are ready to bypass your conscious mind and effectively utilize your subconscious mind when you 1) have a dream clearly in your mind, 2) have taken control of your thoughts, 3) have attached feelings and emotions to your thoughts, 4) have belief in your dream, and 5) are taking action toward your dream. Now, in order to speed up the process of making your dreams come true, follow the easy-to-learn steps to bypass the conscious mind, to lull those guards blocking the entrance to your subconscious.

The power of suggestion causes the subconscious mind to begin its creative work - and here is where the **AFFIRMATIONS** and **REPETITION** play their part. It is the repetition of the same words, the same affirmations that leads to belief; and once that belief becomes a deep conviction, things begin to happen.

This subtle force of the repeated suggestion overcomes your reason, acting directly on your emotions and your feelings, and finally penetrating to the very depths of your subconscious mind. Repetition is the basic principle of all successful advertising.

Pursue the thought of your dream unceasingly. **Repetition** will be the means of driving the suggestion deeply and firmly into the subconscious mind, which will accept and carry out whatever it is powerfully instructed to do. **Repetitive words and phrases said silently or aloud are merely methods of convincing the subconscious mind, because suggestion, no matter what the form, is the way to manifest your dream.**

The subconscious is extremely receptive and can be convinced of the propositions you present to it, be they true or false, positive or negative. Once they are embedded in the subconscious mind, the subconscious goes to work with all of its faculties and energies to materialize your intentions, to make them real in life.

The simpler the words to express the ideas you wish conveyed to the subconscious, the better. If effects are to be permanent, the affirmations must be continued until the desired results are obtained.

Just leave it to the subconscious mind, which has its own ways of making contacts, and of opening doors and avenues that you may never have even thought of. Whatever idea you get, just follow it. Keep a pad and pencil on a stand near the head of your bed, and when these ideas come during the night, note them on a pad.

METHODS TO REACH YOUR SUBCONSCIOUS

- **DEEP BREATHING** is for those who do not have time to incorporate relaxation and visualization into their daily routine. To do this, breath inward while pushing your stomach outward (diaphragmatic breathing) which allows more breath into your lungs. While breathing deeply a few times several times a day, repeat your affirmations and visualize your dream. In addition to your daytime deep breathing, develop the habit of deep breathing to start and end your day--when brushing your teeth in the morning and again at night. Now that it is a habit you will never forget.

- **RELAXATION/VISUALIZATION,** along with affirmations and emotion, is the most effective way to impact your subconscious. Remember, **your subconscious believes what you tell it, especially when the picture is accompanied by emotion.**

Make it a practice to twice daily sit in a quiet place, take a few deep breaths, and allow yourself to totally relax. Concentrate on relaxing your scalp, your forehead, the tiny lines around your eyes, your cheeks, your jaw--allowing your teeth to separate and your tongue to relax. Feel the relaxation flow down into your neck, your shoulders, arms, hands, fingers, into your chest, abdomen, buttocks, thighs, shins, ankles, and toes. From the top of your head to the tips of your toes, allow yourself to totally and completely relax, let go, feel loose and limp--like a rag doll.

As you visualize each part of your body relaxing, you are practicing visualization. **Once you are totally relaxed, see your dream in action.** Look at the details, the time, the smells, the location. Notice how you feel. Play the movie in your mind until you can feel a level of excitement about living the life you desire. When your movie has ended, take three deep breaths and feel the energy flow back into your body, feeling alert and better than ever. This activity, coupled with the twice-daily deep breathing exercises, gives you the opportunity to program your subconscious mind four times a day.

• **HYPNOSIS** is similar to the paragraphs above--relaxation, visualization, affirmations. All hypnosis is self-hypnosis, and if you do the procedure in the preceding two paragraphs, you will experience the results you desire.

CONCLUSION: Success is a journey to a planned destination. Success happens when opportunity meets preparation. Whatever you consider to be a worthy goal or ideal is what defines success for you. When you surround yourself with achievers, you will never have to face difficulties alone. You can always ask for, expect, and receive encouragement and support.

The real starting point is finding your passion, your dream, which is a manifestation of your desire. The more you desire to be a winner, the greater your chance of becoming one. Thoughts have power!

At every stage in your life, what you have or don't have can be directly attributed to the pattern of your thinking. If you see a real need for change, then it is up to you to alter your thought patterns so that you will begin to receive the experiences of the person you have always wanted to be. If you use your imagination, you can possess whatever you desire at this very moment.

Many centuries ago Johann Wolfgang von Goethe said, "Magic is believing in yourself. If you can do that, you can make anything happen." Change your thoughts and you change your world.

WORKSHEET
(In your Journals, answer the following:)

1. **Write out your dream.**

   - What is it?
   - Where are you? Describe your surroundings in detail.
   - Who is there?
   - What are you doing?
   - How do you look? Feel?
   - Can you evoke the wonderful feelings of success?

2. **What are you doing to monitor your thoughts?**

   - Are you using "Cancel-Cancel" for negative thoughts?
   - Have you written affirmations on cards and post it notes?
   - Are you exposed to positive material and people?
   - Do you have a formal reminder twice daily of your dream?

3. **How successful have you been in attaching emotions to your thoughts?**

   - What methods do you use?
   - Do you practice shoulders back, head up and smile?
   - Can you reach within and evoke pleasurable emotions?
   - Do you do this at least twice daily?
   - Do you practice manifesting feelings of wonder, appreciation, gratitude, excitement, reverence, joy and happiness every day?
   - Can you do it?

4. **How strongly do you believe in your dream?**

1 (not much) 3 (average) 5 (tremendous belief)

5. **What action have you taken? What is your level of enthusiasm?**

1 (not much) 3 (average) 5 (tremendous belief)

6. **List your affirmations:**

   -
   -
   -
   -
   -

Gail A. Cassidy

- **Method of bypassing the subconscious:**
- Times a day for deep breathing?
- Times a day for relaxation and visualization?

Schedule for bypassing subconscious: Schedule: Arise, and sitting on the side of the bed, practice deep breathing. Read your dream and review your action steps10 a.m. and 2 p.m. do relaxation and visualization. As you are brushing your teeth, take deep breaths and feel emotions. At bedtime - read dream-visualize it and feel it.

"True happiness comes when you "do" what you're most passionate about." - Cheryl Richardson

What the mind can conceive and believe, it can achieve. -Napoleon Hill

READING RECOMMENDATIONS

Adams, Kathleen. *Journal to the Self: 22 Paths to Personal Growth.* Warner Books.

Allen, Robert. *Multiple Streams of Internet Income* by (or his other book, *Multiple Streams of Income.* Wiley.

Anderson, Nancy. *Work With Passion: How to Do What You Love for a Living.* Carroll & Graf Publishers.

Anthony, Dr. Robert. *Doing What You Love, Loving What You Do.* Berkley Books. (This book is outstanding--timeless and worthy to be on everyone's bookshelf.)

Ballback, Jane Jan Slater. *Unlocking Your Career Potential.* CA: Richard Chang Assoc.

Barrett, James and Geoffrey Williams. *Test Your Own Job Aptitude.* Penguin Books.

Boldt, Laurence. *Zen and the Art of Making a Living.* Penguin.

Bolles, Richard. *What Color Is Your Parachute?* Ten Speed Press.

Breathnache, Sarah. *Simple Abundance.* NY: Warner Books.

Bristol, Claude. *The Magic of Believing* . NY: Cornerstone Library. (1948 and is timeless!)

Bronson, Po. *What Should I Do With My Life?* NY: Random House.

Buzan, Tony. *How to Mind Map.* HarperCollins.

Cameron, Julie. *The Artist's Way: The Spiritual Path to Higher Creativity.* Perigee.

Covey, Stephen. *First Things First.* Simon & Schuster.

Crystal, John & Richard Bolles. *Where Do I Go From Here With My Life?* Ten Speed Press.

Dyer, Wayne. *Real Magic, Erroneous Zones, Believing It is Seeing It, plus all of his books.* Google Wayne Dyer and select from his many offerings.

Edwards, Paul and Sarah. *Finding Your Perfect Work.* NY: Putnam.

Einstein, Patricia. *Intuition, The Path to Inner Wisdom.* MA: Element.

Fisher, Mark. *The Millionaire's Secret.* NY: Fireside.

Gail A. Cassidy

Fortgang Laura Berman. *Living Your Best Life.* NY: Tarcher.

Frankl, Victor. *Man's Search for Meaning.* Beacon Press.

Gelb, Michael. Mindmapping – tape series.

Grabhorn, Lynn. *Excuse Me, Your Life is Waiting.* Hampton Roads.

Haley, Graham. *Haley's Hints.* NAL Trade.

Hill, Napoleon. *Think and Grow Rich.* (San Diego, CA: Aventine Press)

Karbo, Joe. *The Lazy Man's Way to Riches.* Sunset Beach, CA.

Krannich, Ronard and Caryl Rae. *Discover the Right Job for You!* Impact Publications.

Jones, Laurie Beth. *The Path.* NY: Hyperion.

Levoy, Gregg. *Callings, Finding and Following an Authentic Life.* NY: Three Rivers Press.

Pollan, Stephan, *Second Acts.* Colins.

Robbins, Anthony. *Unlimited Power.* Free Press.

Scott, Daniel Dunn. *Interviewing, Building Confidence in Communicating.* Ill.: Foresman & Co.,

Sher, Barbara. *I Would Do What I Love, If Only I Knew What it Was.* Delecorte Press.

"   *Teamworks!* NY: Warner Books.

"   *Wishcraft.* Viking Pres.

Silva, Jose. *Silva Mind Control Method.* NY: Pocket.

Sinatar, Marsha. *Do What You Love, the Money Will Follow.* Dell.

Staples, Walter. *Think Like a Winner!* Pelican.

Waitley, Dennis. *The Psychology of Winning.* Berkley.

Warren, Arnie. *Find Your Passion.* Pallium Books..

Wibbels, Andy. *BlogWild.* Portfolio.

Winter, Barbara. *Making a Living Without a Job.* Bantam Books.

Printed in the United States
By Bookmasters